PRAISE FOR *PUTT*
AGAIN WHEN IT'S A.

Here's a treasure trove of practical biblical wisdom on how to rebuild after your world caves in. When all seems lost, you'll discover hope and encouragement in these pages. Let my friend Tom Holladay be your guide to the comeback that God has in store for you.

LEE STROBEL, bestselling author of *The Case for Christ* and *The Case for Faith*

Life can be complicated, stressful, and painful. That's why I'm so excited about Tom Holladay's new book *Putting It Together Again When It's All Fallen Apart.* Tom shares openly about the wisdom he's learned through tragedy and brokenness in his own life. With grace and compassion, he uses Scriptures, stories, and practical teaching to impart hope and the tools to rebuild after life falls apart.

CRAIG GROESCHEL, pastor of Life.Church and author of *Divine Direction: 7 Decisions That Will Change Your Life*

With God in the picture, nothing is ever too broken to be put back together. But the restoration of a life, a marriage, or a career doesn't just happen. God may provide the power and the plan, but we have to provide the obedience. In *Putting It Together Again When It's All Fallen Apart,* Tom Holladay shines a bright light on the seven steps to restoration found in the powerful story of a biblical hero named Nehemiah. This is a book I encourage you to read.

LARRY OSBORNE, pastor and author, North Coast Church, California

Nothing feels more overwhelming than trying to find hope after experiencing great loss. In *Putting It Together Again When It's All Fallen Apart*, Tom Holladay gives us a powerful blast of hope and a practical biblical guide to finding restoration after loss. We are so thankful for this book and the heart behind it.

KERRY AND CHRIS SHOOK, coauthors of the bestselling *One Month to Live* and founding pastors of Woodlands Church

When life around you feels like it's falling apart, where is the truth that puts us back together again? Time and time again, it's found in Scripture, and Tom Holladay unpacks those truths in such a way that we come face-to-face with God's practical steps. Read this book. It will shepherd your heart and challenge you to pick up the broken pieces of your life and begin building again—but not on your own.

KYLE IDLEMAN, author of *Not a Fan* and *Grace Is Greater*

Tom Holladay knows you don't have to experience a natural disaster to feel like your life has shattered into pieces. In *Putting It Together Again When It's All Fallen Apart*, he shares how to keep your faith and maintain trust in God as you rebuild your life and start again. Drawing on wisdom and fresh insight from the book of Nehemiah, Tom inspires us to embrace the unexpected blessings that come in the midst of unbearable losses.

CHRIS HODGES, senior pastor, Church of the Highlands, and author of *Fresh Air* and *The Daniel Dilemma*

Tom Holladay's strength has been forged out of a life of struggle. In this amazing book, he outlines seven steps to finding strength in the midst of struggle. Step one is finding the strength to start. My prayer is that you'll take the time to read this book! Tom's timeless, Bible-based wisdom will apply to any struggle that has invaded your life. God can use this book to rebuild whatever has been torn down in your life.

MATT BROWN, lead pastor of Sandals Church

There are only two kinds of people: those whose lives have fallen apart and those whose lives will fall apart. I've been there, and I wish I would've had this hope-filled resource. Tom Holladay has written his most important book yet, straight out of his own deeply personal experience. You'll not only be glad you read this, but you'll think of a dozen other people who need it too.

GENE APPEL, senior pastor, Eastside
Christian Church, Anaheim, California

Tom Holladay shares brilliant and practical insights on how to start again, heal, and move forward in faith. He provides profound tools to rebuild your life stronger—on a foundation that lasts. This is an incredible book to read and implement in your life.

JUD WILHITE, senior pastor, Central
Church, and author of *Pursued*

When you're facing a crisis, it can be hard to know what to do and where to begin. Weaving the story of Nehemiah with his own experiences, Tom Holladay will help you work through your difficult circumstances and find hope.

GREG SURRATT, founding pastor of Seacoast Church and
president of ARC (Association of Related Churches)

As members of Saddleback Church, my family has been blessed again and again by Pastor Tom's teaching, and this is Tom Holladay at his absolute best. This book will give you the strength to press on, the will to keep on believing, and a heart that can endure any obstacle. Trust me, you need this book.

> JOHNNIE MOORE, author of *The Martyr's Oath*, founder of The KAIROS Company, and 2017 recipient of the Simon Wiesenthal Center's "medal of valor"

This book is a must-read for anyone who has had or is currently dealing with any kind of hurt or struggle. Let's face it, that's all of us! I love the way Tom Holladay uses Scripture and real-life stories to share God's plan, victories, and healing. My favorite chapter is chapter 5—"Build on your successes."

> JOHN BAKER, Celebrate Recovery founder

Hope is at a premium these days. Tom Holladay shows us what it takes to put hope back in our life when we need it the most. *Putting it Together Again When It's All Fallen Apart* moves rebuilding your life from a good idea to a few powerful but practical steps. We all want to bring about change in our lives, but in this book, Tom shows us how to actually do it.

> TIM HARLOW, senior pastor of Parkview Christian Church, Orland Park, Illinois

Tom Holladay proves throughout this book that he knows Jesus, God's Word, and the longings of people who have had their world flipped upside down. If you or someone you know has ever experienced disappointment (and who hasn't?), then this book will give you answers, hope, and healing. It's easy to read, filled with stories and situations you'll relate to. It's definitely a book you'll want to pass on to a friend.

> DOUG FIELDS, author, pastor, speaker

PUTTING IT TOGETHER AGAIN WHEN IT'S ALL FALLEN APART

7 Principles for Rebuilding Your Life

TOM HOLLADAY

ZONDERVAN

Putting It Together Again When It's All Fallen Apart
Copyright © 2018 by Tom Holladay

Requests for information should be addressed to:
Zondervan, *3900 Sparks Dr. SE, Grand Rapids, Michigan 49546*

ISBN 978-0-310-35039-2 (softcover)

ISBN 978-0-310-35215-0 (audio)

ISBN 978-0-310-35153-5 (ebook)

Cover design: Darren Welch Design, LLC
Cover photos: Shutterstock
Interior design: Kait Lamphere

First printing December 2017 / Printed in the United States of America

CONTENTS

Foreword by Rick Warren 9

1. Find the strength to start 13
   Where to start when you can't find the strength to begin

2. Take the first step 37
   The first step holds the promise of what is to come

3. Appreciate others 55
   The words "thank you" have great power to energize your life

4. Expect and reject opposition 77
   Four common weapons of opposition and four proven steps
   to victory

5. Build on your successes 103
   Success is not a pinnacle to stand on;
   it's a foundation to build on

6. Celebrate to sustain your joy 129
   Intense determination without celebration
   becomes your downfall

7. Dedicate it to God 151
   What is dedicated to God is what will last

Acknowledgments 173
Small Group Study Guide 175

FOREWORD

As a father and now as a grandfather, I've built hundreds of LEGO toy sets with my kids and grandkids. In fact, about two-thirds of our garage space is currently occupied by completed LEGO sets of various kinds: medieval castles, Star Wars, the wild west, pirates, and modern cities. Over the hundreds of hours I've invested in building these sets with my grandkids, I've noticed many parallels to building a strong life. I've even written down my list of "Life Lessons from LEGOs."

Recently, I was moving a nearly three-foot-high LEGO tower to a new spot. It represented days of work, and I was very careful as I moved it. But suddenly, I lost my balance and tipped the tower to one side. From that point, gravity took over! A weak spot was revealed; the building buckled; and it all crashed to the floor, breaking into about five thousand pieces, except for the base that I still held in my hands. My heart sank.

I've had completed projects fall apart before, so I knew a hard truth from experience: *It is far more difficult to rebuild something damaged than to build something new right out of the box, with all the pieces numbered and sorted by bags.*

Yes, it is difficult, but it is *not* impossible! So I knew what I had to do. I picked up the pieces, recommitted to my purpose, and started patiently putting it all back together again with determination.

That may be a metaphor of what you're experiencing as you pick up this book. Your life may seem to be just a jumbled pile of bricks caused by some kind of earthquake in your life, and you're not sure you have the energy or motivation to start putting everything back together again.

Well, as a pastor for more than forty years, let me encourage you with four things about starting over:

First, we all have things fall apart in our lives! *Everybody* does. All of us are broken by something. And having counseled many outwardly successful people, I can tell you that the people who appear to be the most "put together" on the outside are often those who are most falling apart on the inside.

Second, the most heroic stories we all love are about *comebacks*. We admire people who pick themselves up and, with resilience, get back into the game. But have you ever realized that there is no *comeback* without first a *setback*? There is no hero without hardship. It is the struggle that will make you strong. Failure is the pathway to success—*if* you are humble enough to learn the lesson! This book is filled with the lessons you'll need.

Third, when things fall apart, one of the reasons people feel overwhelmed and paralyzed is all the *rubble*. The rubble is all the trash, trivia, and mess that pile up in our lives over time. You have to clear out some rubble before you can rebuild. It's part of the process.

Finally, in order to recover, you'll have to make some tough personal choices, but you won't have to make them by yourself! God and others, particularly those in a church family, can help you with wisdom, perspective, and encouragement. What matters most in rebuilding and recovering from anything is *not* how much money or education or talent you have. What matters most are the choices you make based on the principles you learn. In his book, my dear brother, co-pastor, and friend Tom Holladay lays out these principles with clarity and kindness.

This book is a gold mine of wisdom! If I could, I'd give everyone in the world a copy to read, because we've all faced situations that seemed hopeless. So congratulations! In just picking up this book, you've taken a huge step toward a new you.

Let me encourage you to do four things with this book:

1. Read it slowly. Don't rush it! You need to give God plenty of time to take you through the rebuilding process. Everyone always wants to recover *immediately*. We're more interested in the *speed* of recovery, while God is interested in the *strength* of your foundation so that what you build is stable and lasting. He doesn't want you tipping over so easily.

2. Act on the practical steps suggested at the end of each chapter. In many ways, these pages are the most important in the book. Jesus reminds us at the end of the Sermon on the Mount that it is those who *put his words into practice* who build on a rock-solid foundation (Matthew 7:24).

3. Read this with others. You need support in rebuilding so you don't get discouraged. You're not meant to do this alone. Get one or two other people to read this book with you, and use the questions at the back of the book as a discussion guide.

4. Read this, knowing that God is your dependable source of HOPE! Romans 15:13 reads, "May the God of hope fill you with all joy and peace as you trust in him, so that you may overflow with hope by the power of the Holy Spirit." With God, there is always hope!

For most of my life, I've lived on the coast of California. When the tide is out on a beach, a lot of ugly stuff can be seen. You can see all the driftwood, trash, rocks, and tangled seaweed that have washed up on the shore. There's a lot of rubble when the tide is out. But eventually, the tide *always comes back in.*

The tide may be out in your life right now, and what you are going through doesn't feel good or look good. But this is not the end of your story! The tide always comes back in. Jeremiah 29:11 reads, "'For I know the plans I have for you,' says the LORD. 'They are plans for good and not for disaster, to give you a future and a hope'" (Jeremiah 29:11 NLT). So I urge you to start this journey of rebuilding with renewed hope, expecting God to help you. I'll be praying for you as you read this book. I'm asking God to make the *rest* of your life the *best* of your life. May God bless you!

Dr. Rick Warren
The Purpose Driven Life
Saddleback Church

Chapter 1

FIND THE STRENGTH TO START

Where to start when you can't find the strength to begin

The weaker we feel, the harder we lean. And the harder we lean, the stronger we grow.

Joni Eareckson Tada

Faith is to believe what you do not see; the reward of this faith is to see what you believe.

Augustine

Consider it pure joy, my brothers and sisters, whenever you face trials of many kinds, because you know that the testing of your faith produces perseverance.

James 1:2–3

It was February 20, 1986, in Marysville, California, where I had been pastor to the small congregation of Feather River Baptist Church for five years. My wife, Chaundel, had just finished cleaning our house for a women's ministry meeting, so I decided to take her out for a fine dining experience at Carl's Jr. As we drove over the bridge into town, we noticed that the waters were still filling the river to the very top of the levees. A warm winter rain had hit the nearby Sierra Nevada Mountains, melting much of the snowpack and swelling the lakes and rivers to capacity.

After ordering and sitting down to eat at the restaurant, we saw that people were getting up and leaving in a hurry and went to ask at the counter what was happening.

"A levee broke," we were told, "but you don't have to worry because it's on the other side of the river."

"We *do* have to worry," we said. "We live on that side of the river."

The water rushed through the broken levee and destroyed the mall and businesses that were closest to the break. Then it flooded all that was in its path as it spread through the entire town.

Our home, our church buildings, and many of our members' homes were destroyed, under up to nine feet of water. It's never a good thing to see your house in the lead story for NBC's nightly news program. All Chaundel and I had left were the clothes on our backs and the car we were driving. We drove our Chevy to the levee, and the levee was dry!

It's easier to have some perspective many years later, but I can still remember feeling my hands shake with the adrenaline reaction to a circumstance that immediately changed everything. We had the work of rebuilding our house in front of us. And we had the more difficult work of leading a church of people who all needed to rebuild.

People asked us if we were just going to close the church because the building had been destroyed. Of course not! The church is not a building; it is the people—and thankfully, no one had died in this flood that destroyed so much property.

As I thought about what I would say to encourage these people I loved as they began to rebuild, my mind went to Scripture. The Bible is God's love letter to us, and it shows us how to face the best and the worst of life. I remembered a book in the Bible that is entirely about putting something together again: the book of Nehemiah. Nehemiah was a government leader who rebuilt the wall of Jerusalem after it had fallen into ruin.

As I began to read through this book again with a laser focus on what it taught about how to put things together again, I was amazed at the principles so clearly exemplified by Nehemiah. As these principles began to unfold, I came across Nehemiah 2:20, an encouragement for all who need to rebuild. In that verse, Nehemiah says, "The God of heaven will give us success. We his servants will start rebuilding." This verse became our theme for the next several years.

If you're going to put something together again, you need to know how to fit the pieces. If you're going to rebuild, you must have the right plan, just as much as you needed blueprints to build in the first place. I found that the book of Nehemiah is filled with principles for how to put things together again in a way that will work and how to rebuild in a way that will last.

As I've taught these rebuilding principles in the years since, I've seen people in a wide variety of circumstances find help. You don't have to go through a natural disaster to need to rebuild. For you, putting it together again may mean starting fresh in a career or a relationship. It could just as well involve the need to recover financially, finish a project that's taking too long, restore confidence, renew vision, or face up to some unpleasant task.

It's very likely this kind of change looks impossible to you right now. Things are just too much of a mess for there to be any hope of restoration. We're going to see that Nehemiah had to clear away a lot of rubble before he could start to rebuild the wall! To learn from his example, we will walk through a process that shows how to sort out the possibilities from the rubble.

How do you rebuild what's in ruins? I've talked to many people who have faced such difficult circumstances, and I've found that the emotional energy drain of working to rebuild has often taken them to a place where they can't seem to care. They know they *should* care about starting over, yet just can't find it in them to care anymore.

What Nehemiah teaches us about putting it together again will help you see where to start, even when you can't seem to find the strength to begin. If you already had the energy, you would have started already! God understands that, and he will start with you where you are.

One of the most enriching aspects of looking at the book of Nehemiah is Nehemiah himself. Nehemiah was a man filled with faith—the kind of faith that took action and changed the direction of an entire nation. His faith resulted in the courage to step out, to trust God in prayer, and to find direction for the day-to-day management of problems and opportunities.

Throughout this book, I'll provide a number of opportunities for you to stop and pray. They are there to refresh you for whatever restoration project is in front of you. Since you're in reading mode, it would be easy to skip over these prayers. I'll keep them short so it will be easy for you to pray. Simply read the next few sentences with a prayerful attitude.

Father, I pray that you will use the faith lessons in the book of Nehemiah to put back together what needs to be rebuilt in my life. I ask this in Jesus' name. Amen.

WHERE IT BEGINS

Finding the strength to start is the first step in putting it together again. That strength begins with our reaction to the problem we're facing. Our greatest problem is not our problem; it is how we react to that problem. One of the keys to rebuilding is the way we look at problems.

Your reaction to a problem is determined by the way you see that problem. If you look at a problem and think, *It's a disaster; all is lost*, then your reaction is going to be despair. If you look at a problem and think, *It's unnecessary; that shouldn't have happened*, then your reaction is irritation. If you look at a problem and think, *It's unfair*, then your reaction is anger. If you look at a problem and think, *It's deserved; I did it to myself*, then your reaction is guilt or shame.

There is a better way. We can look at every problem and think, *It's an opportunity to trust God*. Then our reaction is faith. A faith reaction to our problems will radically change the direction of our lives. Warren Wiersbe wrote, "The optimist sees possibilities in the problems, and the pessimist sees problems in the possibilities. One sees the opportunities and the other sees the obstacles. But the real basis for optimism is faith . . . If we see only the problems, we will be defeated; but if we see the possibilities in the problems, we can have victory."[1]

Nehemiah describes the problem he was facing this way: "Those who survived the exile and are back in the province are in great trouble and disgrace. The wall of Jerusalem is broken down, and its gates have been burned with fire" (Nehemiah 1:3). The problem was that the people of God were living in disgrace, and the cause of the problem was that the walls of Jerusalem were in ruins.

In Nehemiah's day, a city's wall was not a decoration; it was its protection. With the walls in ruins, any enemy could easily attack. A city's gates were more than an entrance; they were the civic gathering place—the place where the courts and government met. Without its gates, the city was without leadership.

As Nehemiah faced this problem, he faced the same question all of us face: Will I see only the problem, or will I see the opportunity to trust God in the problem? The Bible clearly shows that our problems are to be seen as opportunities for faith:

- "Dear brothers and sisters, when troubles of any kind come your way, consider it an opportunity for great joy. For you know that when your faith is tested, your endurance has a chance to grow" (James 1:2–3 NLT).
- "For our light and momentary troubles are achieving for us an eternal glory that far outweighs them all" (2 Corinthians 4:17).

---

1. Warren Wiersbe, *The Bumps Are What You Climb On: Encouragement for Difficult Days* (Grand Rapids: Revell, 2006), 125.

- "We also glory in our sufferings, because we know that suffering produces perseverance; perseverance, character; and character, hope" (Romans 5:3–4).

The important question always is, "How do we do this?" Nehemiah models some practical steps we can take to begin to react to problems in a new kind of way.

Reacting in a different way is more than just knowing we should think a certain way. That just creates a feeling of guilt. We find ourselves thinking, *I know I should have more faith, but I don't have more faith, and all I can see is the problem. What's wrong with me?* Nehemiah shares some practical things we can do to get out of that trap of guilt-laden thinking.

We see how Nehemiah began to move from the shock of a problem to a reaction of faith in Nehemiah 1:4: "When I heard these things, I sat down and wept. For some days I mourned and fasted and prayed before the God of heaven."

There are three choices in this verse for beginning to see any problem as an opportunity for faith: mourn, fast, and pray.

- *Mourning* is expressing your hurt to God.
- *Fasting* is focusing your heart on God.
- *Praying* is asking for help from God.

Moving to a place of faith is not accomplished by just flipping a switch. There is a process for beginning to see your problem as an opportunity for faith that includes mourning, fasting, and praying. You cannot choose most of your circumstances, but you can always choose your reaction to those circumstances.

When someone tells you to "just have faith," although you

know they may have your best interests at heart, it can sound like an unreachable platitude. If you could have had faith, you would have had faith, and the words just make you feel guiltier for not having faith! Nehemiah gives us a place to start in the process that gets us to the place of faith when we face a need to rebuild.

MOURNING: Express Your Hurt to God

Nehemiah's immediate reaction to the need to restore the walls was tears. He cried for his city; he cried for God's city.

In 587 BC, Babylon had attacked Jerusalem and destroyed its walls and the temple. All but a few of the people of the southern part of Israel were removed from their land and deported to Babylon, where they suffered in captivity.

Almost fifty years later, in about 538, Persia defeated Babylon, and Cyrus, the king of Persia, began to send some of the people back to Israel. In his first year as king, he sent a group back to rebuild the temple.

Nearly a hundred years later, Nehemiah, an exile from Israel who had risen to become the cupbearer for the current Persian king Artaxerxes, learned that the walls of Jerusalem were still in ruins:

> Hanani, one of my brothers, came from Judah with some other men, and I questioned them about the Jewish remnant that had survived the exile, and also about Jerusalem.
>
> They said to me, "Those who survived the exile and are back in the province are in great trouble and disgrace. The wall of Jerusalem is broken down, and its gates have been burned with fire."

When I heard these things, I sat down and wept. For
some days I mourned and fasted and prayed before the God
of heaven.

Nehemiah 1:2–4

His first reaction was to sit down and weep. But he also had a
continued reaction. He mourned over a period of some days. It only
takes a moment to cry; it takes time to mourn.

The word for "mourning" in the Hebrew language is *abal*. It
carries the idea of showing emotion, expressing it both audibly
and visibly. We need models of how to mourn, and they are found
throughout the Old Testament:

- "Abraham went to mourn for Sarah and to weep over her"
  (Genesis 23:2).
- "Then Jacob tore his clothes, put on sackcloth and mourned
  for his son many days" (Genesis 37:34).
- "When they reached the threshing floor of Atad, near the
  Jordan, they lamented loudly and bitterly; and there Joseph
  observed a seven-day period of mourning for his father"
  (Genesis 50:10).
- "When the whole community learned that Aaron had
  died, all the Israelites mourned for him thirty days"
  (Numbers 20:29).
- "The Israelites grieved for Moses in the plains of Moab thirty
  days, until the time of weeping and mourning was over"
  (Deuteronomy 34:8).
- "When Mordecai learned of all that had been done, he tore
  his clothes, put on sackcloth and ashes, and went out into
  the city, wailing loudly and bitterly" (Esther 4:1).

- "At that time I, Daniel, mourned for three weeks" (Daniel 10:2).

I give these examples because we need some new models for how we mourn. Our culture is not good at mourning, and I know that, as a product of that culture, I'm not good at mourning. I want to mourn too fast and too clean. I want to get back to work as a way to calm the pain instead of taking the time to mourn to begin to heal the pain.

The mourning in these examples is not hidden; it's loud. Putting on sackcloth made it evident to all that they were grieving. Their mourning was not pretty. Mordecai of the book of Esther is a mentor for all mourners. Like Nehemiah, he saw what began in mourning save a nation. His mourning was not dignified, but it was honest. It came with the rough texture of sackcloth and the black streaks of bitter tears running through the ashes that covered his face.

You see examples in the Old Testament of mourning that lasted seven days (Genesis 50:10), thirty days (Numbers 20:29), and even seventy days (Genesis 50:3–4). It takes time to mourn. You can't do it in an instant.

Is there a hurt or a loss you've never taken the time to mourn? You may have faced this hurt many years ago, or you may be facing it right now. There are huge hurts of life and the day-by-day hurts of life, and with both of them, you need to take time to mourn.

Have you taken the time to mourn the loss of that important relationship? Or are you hiding from the hurt in your hurry?

You may be getting older and don't have the physical energy you used to have. Have you taken time to mourn that loss? Or are you just sort of irritated about it all the time?

Here's why this is so important: *If you don't take the time to mourn, you can't see the opportunity in the problem, because you will never see past the hurt.* What is it that you need to take the time to mourn?

You may think, *But that will make me sad.* Sadness is not a bad thing. There are some things in life that need to be mourned. Our culture of denial says sadness is always bad, but that is just simply not true. In fact, the sadness of mourning brings one of God's greatest gifts into our lives.

I was recently preparing a funeral message for a family who had lost their young mom in heartbreaking circumstances and was searching my mind for how to express God's hope to them. As I was considering what to say, I felt God impressing me to not talk to them about hope, but to encourage them to mourn. Jesus taught us, "Blessed are those who mourn, for they will be comforted" (Matthew 5:4). Our mourning brings the gift of God's comfort, a gift that often comes only through our mourning. By not taking the time to mourn, we are missing out on the comfort our Father wants to give.

One of the most important things to learn about mourning is that we all grieve in different ways. Some need to talk; some need to be quiet. Some have a flood of tears; others feel a dearth of emotion. I have learned that our grief is one of the most individual things about us. Grief is like our fingerprints—unique to every one of us.

Some who don't understand this are reluctant to mourn because they feel pressed to mourn like others, in a way that doesn't fit their unique personality. Let me say clearly that I'm not telling you *how* to mourn; I'm simply encouraging you to *take the time* to mourn in a way that fits you.

Mourning expresses honest grief over what has been lost. Seeing the opportunity in any problem begins by being able to say there is a problem. There is a form of Christian denial that wants to skip this step. Some Christians pretend that because God works within their problems, there is no loss in them. It's a shortcut that short-circuits the work God needs to do in our souls if we are to truly rebuild.

In the Japanese art form kintsugi, a broken pot is repaired with glue that is infused with gold dust. The result is veins of gold where the vase has been put back together. The vase has still been broken, yet it now has a beauty it did not have before. It often has an even greater value than it had before.

It's enticing to say this shows that when something has been broken, it is now all the better for it. This is not about "better" or "worse"; it's about working with the reality of something that has been broken. "Better" and "worse" thinking can be our greatest enemy when we are seeking to put something together again.

This is because we all know deep inside that it would have been better if it had not been broken in the first place. If that awful thing hadn't happened. If those words had not been said. If we had only done something different. The ultimate in this "better" or "worse" thinking is that it would have been better if Adam and Eve had not sinned in the garden. But they did sin, as any of us would have. And so we live in a broken world.

Instead of chasing the false picture that it's better to be broken, let kintsugi illustrate the truth that God is a master craftsman in working with what is broken. Embrace the reality revealed in 2 Corinthians 4:7 (NLT) that we are clay pots: "We now have this light shining in our hearts, but we ourselves are like fragile clay jars containing this great treasure. This makes it clear that our great power is from God, not from ourselves."

God invites us to focus not on the clay jar, but on what he has put into the jar. Yes, the jar is fragile and easily broken. And yes, God has poured his love and grace into that very jar. As we see this truth more and more, we'll find that we are relying less on a need to convince ourselves that "it's really better this way," and more on the power of God that is at work, even with what has been broken.

FASTING: Focus Your Heart on God

Nehemiah teaches us to fast to help us focus our attention on God as we consider our need to put something together again. The idea of fasting, or abstaining from food for a time, may be unfamiliar to you. Let's take a very brief look at what the Bible teaches about fasting.

Fasting is always accompanied by prayer in the Scriptures. Two examples among many are Anna of the Christmas story and the early church in Antioch.

> Then she [Anna] lived as a widow to the age of eighty-four. She never left the Temple but stayed there day and night, worshiping God with fasting and prayer.
>
> **Luke 2:37 NLT**

> Paul and Barnabas appointed elders for them in each church and, with prayer and fasting, committed them to the Lord, in whom they had put their trust.
>
> **Acts 14:23**

The attitude behind fasting is humility. In preparation for the return of the Israelites to Jerusalem, Ezra the priest leads the people to fast "so that we might humble ourselves before our God" (Ezra 8:21). Jesus warns us in the Sermon on the Mount about fasting to impress others: "Be careful not to practice your righteous-ness in front of others to be seen by them. If you do, you will have no reward from your Father in heaven" (Matthew 6:1). You don't fast to get others' attention on you; you fast to get your attention on God.

People fasted for different reasons—sometimes to express grief (2 Samuel 1:11), sometimes to express repentance (Jonah 3:4–5; Daniel 9:3–6), sometimes to earnestly ask for God's help (2 Chronicles 20:2–4), and sometimes as an expression of worship and fellowship with God (Luke 2:36–37; Acts 13:1–2).

Reading through these verses shows that fasting is not just a change in diet; it is a change in activity that prompts a change in heart. The value of fasting is not in what we *aren't* doing—namely, eating; it's in what we *are* doing—namely, focusing on God.

The purpose of fasting is not self-denial. In fact, focusing merely on denying ourselves food or drink has no spiritual benefit and often results in pride: "These rules may seem wise because they require strong devotion, pious self-denial, and severe bodily discipline. But they provide no help in conquering a person's evil desires" (Colossians 2:23 NLT).

The value of fasting is that it opens up space for focusing on God. If you don't focus your attention on God, you will find yourself either narrowing the picture or blurring the picture. You narrow the picture when all you see is the problem. Focusing on God helps you see the greatness of God as you face a need to rebuild. You blur the picture when you become so overwhelmed that you try to escape the problem or live in denial that there is a problem. There are a lot of busy people trying to escape problems. Focusing your attention on God gives the spiritual strength to face the reality of the difficulty.

Just wanting to focus more on God is not enough. We need to do something practical that will change our focus. People are not like cameras; we don't have autofocus! We must intentionally focus, and fasting helps us do that. Fasting is an intentional change of perspective as we focus on God.

Here's a simple place to start: try a one-meal fast. If you never eat breakfast, that doesn't count! Take a meal you usually eat and use that time to fix your attention on God. For instance, skip a lunch and take that thirty minutes or hour to focus your attention on God with that hurt you've been facing. If you have dietary issues, please check with your doctor first.

PRAYER: Ask for Help from God

To react to a problem in a way that helps you see the opportunity for faith, you mourn, you fast, and then you pray.

It's important to note that prayer is the third thing Nehemiah does. Before he prays, he takes time to mourn and fast. He takes some time to express his heart and to experience the presence of God before he begins to pray.

If you feel like you don't have anything to say when you sit down to pray, the best thing to do is to not say anything. Sit in God's presence and silently mourn the loss. That will lead to a place where you can pray.

What a prayer Nehemiah prays! He gives us a model of four specific ways to pray that will help you recognize God's opportunities for faith in the midst of your problems. We're letting Nehemiah guide us through what to do in the process of rebuilding, so I encourage you to pray these prayers as you read them.

The prayer that strengthens you to see the opportunity for faith as you rebuild begins by *recognizing who God is*:

"LORD, the God of heaven, the great and awesome God, who keeps his covenant of love with those who love him and keep his commandments, let your ear be attentive and your eyes open to hear the prayer your servant is praying before you day and night for your servants, the people of Israel."

Nehemiah 1:5–6

Nehemiah prays to God as "the great and awesome God." Recognize that God is all-powerful when you pray—especially in the midst of a problem.

Then he prays, "Who keeps his covenant of love." God is all-powerful, and he is also faithful. We can count on him to keep his promises. God never promised us no problems in this world; he promised just the opposite. He tells us we will face trials. God promises hope in the midst of problems. God has promised deliverance one day from all of our problems.

Then he prays, "Let your ear be attentive and your eyes open." God is aware of your need. His eyes are wide open. His ears are always attentive. He knows exactly what you're going through. When you remind yourself of this in prayer, you are reminding yourself of the truth of who God is.

About a week after the flood that destroyed our church and homes, a few dozen members of our small church gathered at Mary Lou's house to pray together. It would be our first meeting together as a church after the dispersal and confusion of the flood. Although I would be leading the prayer meeting, I honestly didn't know what to expect.

My fear was that our anxiety over our circumstances would overwhelm our feeble attempts at prayers. Instead, as we quietly voiced our trust in God's goodness and faithfulness, we felt our faith being built in ways I can only describe as miraculous. We walked from that room with the same circumstances as when we had walked in, but with our faith soaring to heights that carried us through the rebuilding.

If only every prayer meeting were like this. For every experience like this, I can count dozens upon dozens where we were faithful to pray but felt very little new strength as we prayed those prayers. I've come to see that even in those times when we may not feel the power of the prayer, the prayer is working just as powerfully.

When we focus on the character and greatness of God rather than just reciting our worries, we will often find new strength coming in the moment of our prayers.

The fact that we may or may not feel an emotional burst of strength in the moment of prayer often has little to do with the real strength that God gives the next hour or day in the moment of need.

The prayer that helps you to see the opportunity for faith as you face a problem first recognizes who God is. Second, it *recognizes who you are*. Nehemiah prays, "I confess the sins we Israelites, including myself and my father's family, have committed against you. We have acted very wickedly toward you. We have not obeyed the commands, decrees and laws you gave your servant Moses" (Nehemiah 1:6–7).

Nehemiah is open with God about the sins not only of the nation but also of himself and his family. Problems are present in this world, *not* because of who God is, but because we trust ourselves instead of God. It began with Adam and Eve in the Garden of Eden, and we're still bringing those problems into life today.

Our sin causes us to have shame over the problems we know are our fault, and blame over the problems we consider to be someone else's fault. Admitting this painfully obvious truth that we resort to shame and blame is often the key to breaking through the problem and getting to a place where we can have faith.

We all have sinful selfishness in our lives. Sometimes we see it, and sometimes we don't. It's refreshing to sit in God's presence and say, "I know some of the selfishness that is in my life, but also know there is much I don't see. I confess what I do know, and I thank you for loving me." This honest confession has the power to move us from a place of shame or blame to a place of faith. It moves us from focusing on what we deserve to focusing on God's undeserved grace.

Third, if you want to have faith in the midst of your problems, you have to *call on the promises of God*. Nehemiah offers this prayer:

> "Remember the instruction you gave your servant Moses, saying, 'If you are unfaithful, I will scatter you among the nations, but if you return to me and obey my commands, then even if your exiled people are at the farthest horizon, I will gather them from there and bring them to the place I have chosen as a dwelling for my Name.'
>
> "They are your servants and your people, whom you redeemed by your great strength and your mighty hand."
>
> **Nehemiah 1:8–10**

Nehemiah found a specific promise for his situation from the Old Testament, and he spoke it out as he prayed. He remembered with God the promise that even if the people were exiled, God would gather them if they would only return to him.

Instead of looking for hope in his circumstances, Nehemiah looked for hope in the promises of God. You cannot depend on your circumstances. It may seem you can when your circumstances are going well, but then they turn against you. I've often benefited from what David Henderson wrote about circumstances:

> If there was a police lineup of all that had ever robbed anyone of hope, certainly the most fingered culprit would be that foul menace called Circumstance. *Circumstantia* means "stand around." The word points to those events and people that crowd in around us, loitering in the halls of our lives and blocking the view out the window to the broader reality beyond . . .
>
> When positive circumstances crowd around us, we are tempted to deposit our hope in them, not the Lord. The stock market climbs, and our portfolio grows. We tiptoe our way through some tough circumstances and come out unscathed . . . How tempting it is to believe that circumstances like these are solid enough to stand on, to bear the weight of our confidence, our identity, or our future . . .
>
> Negative circumstances are equally adept at crowding out our view of deeper realities. When illness strikes, we cannot look beyond the pain. Grief blocks the view when a loved one dies, embarrassment clouds our vision when we are fired from a job, weariness and resentment get in our way when we care for an aging parent, and loneliness crowds the window when an engagement falls through . . .
>
> Despair says circumstances tell us what is true about God. Hope says God tells us what is true about circumstances.[2]

---

2. David W. Henderson, "Hope: Anchoring Your Heart to a Sure and Certain Future," *Discipleship Journal* 114 (November/December 1999), www.angelfire.com/jazz/karen_trust/OursChrist/Anchor1.html (accessed July 6, 2017).

A great opportunity presents itself when circumstances betray you—the opportunity to depend on God's great promises. Nehemiah teaches us how to take the most important step in depending on God's promises. He found a specific promise that fit the circumstance he was facing. The more specific the promise, the more your faith is strengthened.

To find that promise, look in the Bible—as Nehemiah did. It is filled with the promises of God; one writer has counted more than eight thousand.[3] How do you find the one you need amid all the verses in the Bible? Maybe you'll be successful by doing a search on the web to find it, but I've found that's not the way it usually happens. God typically takes us through a process of searching. It could be through studying the Bible, listening to a message, or talking to another believer. When we discover a promise through this process, it's like finding buried treasure.

When our home and church were destroyed by a flood, I needed a promise for my own life, and as a young pastor, I wanted to give hope to our church. I began to read through the book of Nehemiah, since I knew it was about rebuilding, and I came across the promise we looked at earlier from Nehemiah 2:20: "We his servants will start rebuilding."

Those words hit me like an electric jolt; it was just the promise I needed. In my searching, God gave me a promise I will treasure for the rest of my life. This process of searching starts with prayer. Ask God what *specific promise* he has for the problem you are facing as you begin your search.

Nehemiah's final lesson on prayer for those who would rebuild is to *ask for specific help as you pray*: "Lord, let your ear be attentive

---

3. Herbert Lockyer, *All the Promises of the Bible* (Grand Rapids: Zondervan, 1990).

to the prayer of this your servant and to the prayer of your servants who delight in revering your name. Give your servant success today by granting him favor in the presence of this man" (Nehemiah 1:11). Nehemiah specifically asks for success as he prepares to go to make a request of the king.

Notice that this is a prayer with a schedule—"give your servant success today." And it's a prayer with a plan—"favor in the presence of this man." Nehemiah asks specifically for what he needs and specifically for when he needs it.

Sometimes we try to do God a favor by being very general with our prayers: "God, if you want to give success someday, I pray that one day you might give whatever success you want to give, unless you don't want to give it."

We don't want to be presumptive in God's presence, so we over-react by not asking for anything at all. Ask specifically! The Holy Spirit will often motivate specific prayers for God's will to be done in your life. And if you are specifically wrong in what you request, God will specifically redirect your heart.

I encourage you to put these four lessons on praying with faith into practice by praying right now:

Father, I offer you praise in the midst of this problem. You are greater than any problem I am facing. You are a great and awesome God. Keep me aware of your unfailing love and your faithful working out of your plan. I confess the sin I am aware of, and I thank you for the forgiveness you've given in Christ. I ask you to lead me in searching for a promise to hold on to. Finally, here are my practical requests for what I'm asking you to do and when I'm asking you to do it as I face this need to rebuild. In Jesus' name I pray. Amen.

FIND THE STRENGTH TO START:
My First Steps

MOURNING: Express your hurt to God

Write down some of the ways you have expressed your hurt to God—or plan to express your hurt. Some people are helped by journaling, others by solitude. Some best express their hurt sitting in a comfortable place, others while walking. Some need to express their heart to God in silence; others will express their heart out loud. Listening to music can speak to your heart in ways that nothing else can. Here is a list of songs you may want to listen to:

SONGS FOR THE HURTING

Kari Jobe—"I Am Not Alone"

Steven Curtis Chapman—"Jesus Will Meet You There"

Plumb—"Need You Now (How Many Times)"

Laura Story—"Blessings"

Meredith Andrews—"Not for a Moment"

Jeremy Camp—"He Knows"

Lauren Daigle—"Trust in You"

Casting Crowns—"Just Be Held"

For King and Country—"Busted Heart (Hold On to Me)"

Pam Thum—"Life Is Hard (God Is Good)"

Sara Groves—"He's Always Been Faithful"

Matt Maher—"Lord, I Need You"

JJ Heller—"Your Hands"

Building 429—"No One Else Knows"

Meredith Andrews—"Hands That Are Holding Me"

All Sons and Daughters—"Great Are You, Lord"

Danny Gokey—"Tell Your Heart to Beat Again"

Audrey Assad—"Good to Me"

MercyMe—"The Hurt and the Healer"

Tommy Walker—"When I Don't Know What to Do"

Ginny Owens—"If You Want Me To"

Matt Redman—"Blessed Be Your Name"

Phil Wickham—"Safe"

Steven Curtis Chapman—"Hallelujah, You Are Good"

Third Day—"Cry Out to Jesus"

Shane & Shane—"Though You Slay Me"

Nichole Nordeman and Erin O'Donnell—"You Are Good"

You can download this as a Spotify playlist at
http://sptfy.com/Y2u.

FASTING: Focus your heart on God

Write down your date for a day of fasting.

Decide if you're going to do a one-meal fast, a juice fast (in which you drink juice instead of eat food for each meal), or a day-long fast. You may need to check with your doctor, and you should always drink water when you fast.

Take the time you would have eaten to focus on God in silence, prayer, or reading.

Remember that your greatest benefit from fasting may come not on the day you fast but on the days that follow.

PRAYER: Ask for help from God

Make plans to take the step of talking to God about what you need to put together again, whether it's in an extended time of prayer or in a brief daily prayer time.

Use Nehemiah's simple outline to direct your prayers:

- Recognize who God is.
- Recognize who you are.
- Call on God's promises.
- Ask for specific help.

Chapter 2

TAKE THE FIRST STEP

The first step holds the promise
of what is to come

Faith is taking the first step, even when you don't see the whole staircase.

Martin Luther King Jr.[1]

The greatest waste of time is the waste of time in getting started.

Dawson Trotman

For I can do everything through Christ, who gives me strength.

Philippians 4:13 NLT

---

1. "MLK Quote of the Week: 'Faith Is Taking the First Step,'" King Center, February 21, 2013, www.thekingcenter.org/blog/mlk-quote-week-faith-taking-first-step (accessed August 16, 2017).

Although Julie and Chad still lived under the same roof, the unspoken understanding that their marriage had ended pervaded the walls of their home. The technical details of separation and divorce were still to come, but they had both accepted the reality of a failed relationship.

There had been no single event that had brought their marriage to this point. Instead, they had just gradually begun to live separate lives. Julie's focus on building a business and Chad's goals for building a career left no time for their relationship. The result has happened in thousands of relationships. With no time together, they came to feel they no longer needed the other in their life.

They did not know it yet, but just as they had gradually grown apart, they were about to begin to gradually grow together again. It began with an invitation to Julie to give some free consultation on the needs of small business owners to a group at Saddleback Church.

"I'm not a churchgoer or believer in all that," she told them.

"Your opinion is exactly the one we need," they replied.

She went once and told herself she had fulfilled her responsibility. But they asked her back and kept asking until she agreed. Over the next few months as she gave advice, she also felt her heart being drawn to the faith she saw in some of the people in the group. Julie began a relationship with Christ and knew immediately that everything had changed.

Without thinking what it might mean for their relationship, she knew she had to share what she had found with Chad. He needed the hope, peace, and joy she was now beginning to experience. She asked him to go with her to church, and at first, he said he didn't really feel a need for that. But as he began to see a change in her life and she continued to ask from time to time, he finally said yes.

As they drove to church for the first time together, Chad felt overwhelmed by the size of the church. They passed by a tram taking families from a lower parking lot to the children's building, and that did it. "This isn't church; it's Disneyland," Chad said. They drove straight out of the parking lot without even stopping.

Julie was saddened, yet still felt compelled to let Chad in on what God was doing in her life. She found out there was a smaller worship service at Saddleback, and asked Chad if he might be willing to try that. Again, he said yes—and this time when they went, they stayed.

Chad saw what had been so meaningful to Julie, and he also decided to begin a relationship with Jesus. As two new believers, they now had the somewhat scary opportunity to see what this might mean for their marriage.

It's vital to pause a moment to recognize that none of this would have happened without someone taking the first step. Julie connected with a church because someone asked and kept asking. Then Julie kept asking Chad to begin to see with her the difference that Jesus could make. For this relationship to be restored, someone needed to ask. And then ask again.

This is the crucial moment when a person is rebuilding. Unless someone *initiates a first step*, there will be no chance to begin again.

Suppose you're at the start of a hundred-meter race. You're settled in the blocks; the starter's pistol is about to fire. But instead of thinking about the race, you're considering every detail of the last race you ran. You're not intently listening for the gun, so of course you're not going to get started well. To start well, every fiber of your being must be listening for that starter's pistol.

To rebuild well you must start well. How do you become the kind of person who initiates action? How do you get that relationship, career, plan, or project out of the starting blocks?

Nehemiah gives great encouragement for getting things started. He decides to begin the rebuilding of Jerusalem's walls and finds that everybody is just standing around, shaking their heads, and essentially saying, "This is terrible; this is awful." From this group of nonstarters, he gets things started by making four decisions. These decisions caused him to be an initiator when everybody else was just a spectator. They are simple decisions—decisions you can make, beginning right now.

DECIDE TO TAKE A STAND

Look at how the story unfolds in Nehemiah 2:1–5:

> In the month of Nisan in the twentieth year of King Artaxerxes, when wine was brought for him, I took the wine and gave it to the king. I had not been sad in his presence before, so the king asked me, "Why does your face look so sad when you are not ill? This can be nothing but sadness of heart."
>
> I was very much afraid, but I said to the king, "May the king live forever! Why should my face not look sad when the city where my ancestors are buried lies in ruins, and its gates have been destroyed by fire?"
>
> The king said to me, "What is it you want?"

Then I prayed to the God of heaven, and I answered the king, "If it pleases the king and if your servant has found favor in his sight, let him send me to the city in Judah where my ancestors are buried so that I can rebuild it."

Nehemiah gets things started by talking to the king. He knows that to move ahead he has to have the king's support. The king will have to allow him to go and provide him the resources.

Nehemiah said, "I was very much afraid." What was he afraid of? This was much more than fear of public speaking. In that day, if you asked something of a king and he denied your request, it came with a severe consequence. Kings did not like disgruntled subjects in their kingdom, so if they denied a request, they also cut off your head— which ensured there were no unhappy subjects walking around!

To put something together again, you will have to face your fears. One of our greatest fears is the fear of opening ourselves up to further pain. To even think about rebuilding means we are taking the risk of disappointment if it doesn't work. It seems safer to just accept the failure and move on.

The only way to move past that fear is found in 1 John 4:18: "There is no fear in love. But perfect love drives out fear, because fear has to do with punishment. The one who fears is not made perfect in love." Love is God's antidote to fear. God's love for you is the way to see past your fear.

John says that "fear has to do with punishment." Fear tells us that the circumstances and people in our lives are out to punish us when we take a risk. Fear causes us to take the pain in our lives personally, as if we deserve nothing but punishment. Apart from God's love, this would be true, but in God's grace, we are given nothing but love.

So now you can take God's love personally. You can know that whatever risk you take, he is working to bless you and not to punish you. You can know that no matter what the result of the stand you take is, God will stand with you.

To initiate faith for what God wants done, there must be someone with the courage to take a stand. David exemplified it with Goliath; Deborah showed it when she led Israel to victory; and Paul evidenced it as he preached to the Gentiles.

In history, you see this courage in Martin Luther's famous statement "Here I stand; I cannot do otherwise, so help me God," as he defended the truths that ignited the Reformation. Martin Luther King Jr. quoted those words in his "Letter from a Birmingham Jail" as he took his own stand for racial equality.[2] Catherine Booth drew on those words as she said, "Here I stand and make my boast, that the Christ of God, my Christ, the Christ of the Salvation Army, does meet this crying need of the soul, does fill this aching void."[3] As cofounder of the Salvation Army, she was standing for the power of Christ to meet the needs of social injustice in her day.

These are people who took a stand when no one else would take a stand. They show that taking a stand means having the courage to face the consequences. Whether you're snickered at, stared at, shouted at, or shot at, there will be consequences when you take a stand, because you are the one leading the way.

Intuitively we all know there will be pressure that comes with taking a stand. That's why it's hard to do.

This is true even if it's a stand you take within your own heart. You decide, *I'm going to take a stand against this laziness in my life.*

---

2. Martin Luther King Jr., "Letter from a Birmingham Jail," April 16, 1963, www.africa.upenn.edu/Articles_Gen/Letter_Birmingham.html (accessed July 6, 2017).

3. Mrs. Booth, *Popular Christianity: A Series of Lectures* (London: Salvation Army, 1887), 6.

I'm going to restore a life of living for God's purpose. Even before you tell anyone else, this internal stand brings the pressure of needing to live a different way. You are no longer coasting downhill; you've changed direction and are headed uphill.

I asked Julie what gave her the courage to continue to take the first steps to ask Chad to come to church with her. "It was very scary for me," she said, "because I didn't want him to think I was trying to change him." For her, the courage came each time she discovered a life-changing truth in the Bible. It wasn't about her trying to change him, but about the ways God was changing her.

Chad, of course, had to have the courage to say yes, even after he had said no. To let go of a no takes a great deal of humility. For him, it came out of a desire to restore their relationship. "Even though we didn't like each other at that point," he said, "I had married her because I loved her. So I was willing to try anything, and what I had been trying didn't seem to be working." It takes great courage to admit that what you've been trying isn't working and to try something different!

Jesus Christ can give you the courage to take that stand. He took a stand for you. He went to the cross for you and gave himself for your sin. Don't try to take the stand in your strength. There is no greater encouragement I can give than to urge you to take your stand in the strength that Jesus can give you. Ask him for that strength right now.

DECIDE TO PREPARE FOR SUCCESS

The king said yes, and Nehemiah was ready for the king to say yes. He prepared in advance for what might happen if the king was favorable to his request:

Then the king, with the queen sitting beside him, asked me, "How long will your journey take, and when will you get back?" It pleased the king to send me; so I set a time.

I also said to him, "If it pleases the king, may I have letters to the governors of Trans-Euphrates, so that they will provide me safe-conduct until I arrive in Judah? And may I have a letter to Asaph, keeper of the royal park, so he will give me timber to make beams for the gates of the citadel by the temple and for the city wall and for the residence I will occupy?" And because the gracious hand of my God was on me, the king granted my requests.

Nehemiah 2:6–8

Nehemiah's preparation began even as he made his request. Notice that the king had the queen sitting beside him. Nehemiah likely knew that the king would be more open to his request with the queen present, perhaps because of the favor he enjoyed with the queen due to his role in protecting the king. We prepare for success by making our requests at the right time.

We also prepare for success by being ready to move forward. So often we allow ourselves to become so worried about somebody saying no that we give no thought to what we're going to do if they happen to say yes. Nehemiah had wisely spent his energy focusing on what he was going to do when the king said yes.

There's a principle here: *People who get things started prepare for success rather than worry about failure.* Are you spending most of your energy readying yourself for failure or preparing yourself for success?

One of the ways to prepare is to make a simple list of what you need. When the king asked what he could do, Nehemiah had a list of the resources he would need and the people who could help. To be a person who gets things done, you must get that list in your mind before the door of opportunity opens, so that when it opens, you're immediately ready to walk through it.

There is sometimes great faith in a simple list of needs. In the flood we experienced, the water level in our home went to nine feet. Our first step in rebuilding was to strip our home down to the subfloor and studs by tearing up all of the flooring and removing all of the wallboard.

I feel deep gratitude for the great help my wife's parents, Jimmy and Dot, provided in our rebuilding. Jimmy had done a great deal of construction work as a missionary builder of churches, and one of the first things he did was to make a list of the materials we'd need to rebuild. We were just starting to recover and didn't have resources to buy those materials, but he still started a list.

One day he counted that we would need ninety-eight sheets of wallboard to repair the house. That very night, someone from out of town visited our home to see the damage. Shaking his head after looking at it all, he asked, "Is there anything I can do to help?"

"Yes," said Jimmy, "we need ninety-eight sheets of wallboard!" That man bought the wallboard for us to rebuild our home because Jimmy had prepared in advance for someone to say yes. Rebuilders plan for success.

Where do you need to stop worrying about failure and start preparing for success? You may want to stop right now and write down a list of the resources you need to begin again.

DECIDE TO REVIEW THE PROBLEM

The next step Nehemiah takes to get things started is to undertake a firsthand review of the problem:

I went to Jerusalem, and after staying there three days I set out during the night with a few others. I had not told anyone what my God had put in my heart to do for Jerusalem. There were no mounts with me except the one I was riding on.

By night I went out through the Valley Gate toward the Jackal Well and the Dung Gate, examining the walls of Jerusalem, which had been broken down, and its gates, which had been destroyed by fire.

Nehemiah 2:11–13

I realize the main thing you may have noticed in this passage are the words "Dung Gate." Why would they have a dung gate? Dung happens—that's all we need to say about that.

The significant thing that happens here is Nehemiah's personal and detailed review of the problem. He went through each gate, and he looked at each wall. This was not something he could delegate to someone else or leave to another's opinion. He needed to see for himself exactly where the breaks in the wall were and what needed to be done to rebuild.

Nehemiah teaches us something very important about those who get things started. Instead of sitting around and moping about the unknown and unseen, those who initiate actions of faith face a problem head-on. There are a number of valuable aspects to a firsthand review of the problem.

First, a personal review *cuts the problem down to a manageable size.* When I saw pictures of our home and church underwater on the front pages of newspapers and as the lead story on national news, recovery looked impossible. It looked like a disaster from which we would never rebuild. But when I got into a boat with my friend

Bob and rowed out to see our homes and the church, I could start to see how we could rebuild. It looked like there was a lot of work to be done, but it no longer looked impossible. The furniture was tossed and jumbled, but it was still our furniture. We had a few feet of water in the house, but it was still our house. Looking at the problem can cut it down to manageable size. Face the problem, and there's every possibility that God's going to show you how to manage the solution.

Second, a firsthand review of the problem *gives a sense of the immediate need*. Sometimes we procrastinate by mentally sticking the problem off in a corner. When we do that, the problem usually doesn't just go away; it often grows larger through a lack of attention. And in the back of our minds, there is a gnawing anxiety about the problem we're ignoring that saps our energy.

When we face the problem, we see the immediacy of the need in a way that motivates us to take the first step. We move from a fuzzy feeling of "I really should do something about this" to a concrete decision to act.

A third benefit of a firsthand review is that it *renews a spirit of personal responsibility*. When we're not looking at the problem, it feels like someone out there somewhere is taking care of it. Everybody's responsibility is nobody's responsibility. When we face the problem, we feel the responsibility for taking action. It's amazing how many problems still exist because we're pretending that someone else will do something.

Sometimes the person we're pretending will do something is God. I want to be extremely careful here in saying that in the end *it is God* who does all the work. What we sometimes miss is that in the work he is doing, he has something for us to do. A firsthand review of the problem will help us see where God wants us to act.

We can certainly rush ahead when God wants us to wait. I want to deal here with the opposite problem, namely, thinking it is spiritual to just wait when God has something for us to do. Even as great a man of faith as Moses faced this problem. When the people of Israel were trapped between the Red Sea and the Egyptian army, Moses told the people, "Do not be afraid. Stand firm and you will see the deliverance the LORD will bring you today. The Egyptians you see today you will never see again. The LORD will fight for you; you need only to be still" (Exodus 14:13–14).

Moses's words sound so trusting and spiritual. They were also exactly wrong. God immediately says to Moses, "Why are you crying out to me? Tell the Israelites to move on. Raise your staff and stretch out your hand over the sea to divide the water so that the Israelites can go through the sea on dry ground" (Exodus 14:15–16). Moses was telling them to stand still when God wanted them to move ahead!

While it certainly requires great discernment to figure out when we should wait and do nothing and when we should move ahead, I have observed that more times than we'd like to admit, we face the same problem Moses did that day. God is telling us to act, and we are hiding behind spiritual-sounding words.

I like the example of the apostle Paul, one of the greatest initiators of all history. He was the first to start churches all over the known world. Paul had a habit of moving ahead in whatever direction he felt God might be leading. If a door was open, he kept moving; if it was closed, he stopped or was redirected. God is often better able to work with us when we're moving than when we're stalled and he's trying to get us moving.

As you review the problem, a good prayer to pray is, "God, what do you want me to do next?"

DECIDE TO ASK FOR HELP

The fourth decision that Nehemiah made in initiating change was the decision to involve others and ask for help:

> Then I said to them, "You see the trouble we are in: Jerusalem lies in ruins, and its gates have been burned with fire. Come, let us rebuild the wall of Jerusalem, and we will no longer be in disgrace." I also told them about the gracious hand of my God on me and what the king had said to me.
>
> They replied, "Let us start rebuilding." So they began this good work.
>
> **Nehemiah 2:17–18**

Every person down through history who has been an effective initiator has asked for help. Initiators are not independent. Without help, Nehemiah would have just been a lone crusader, but with help, he rebuilt the wall. Rebuilding a building, career, relationship, marriage, or ministry takes a lot of hard work. So those who face the task of rebuilding need help—carpenters to rebuild a house, counseling to restore a marriage, training to renew a career.

Here is a simple principle of life: *To get help, you have to ask for help.* Help doesn't come without asking. We think it should—that people will just notice and show up and help. It doesn't happen that way. Even God asks us to ask so that he will help us in our lives: "Ask and it will be given to you" (Matthew 7:7).

Some people are good at asking for help, but most of us are not. Most of the time, we'd rather do it ourselves. It may be a matter of pride, but just as often it's that we don't want to bother other people. We tell ourselves they have important things going on in their lives.

But the truth of the matter is *we need each other's help*. One of the important things in their lives is you!

When I faced the challenge of rebuilding a house and church, I had to make a decision: Was I going to try to do it alone? If I had, the job never would have been completed and my life would have taken a turn toward the bitterness and loneliness that grow out of failing alone.

One month before the flood hit, I had seen a news report about Gordon Bushnell's highway in Minnesota. Bushnell believed there should be a highway between Duluth, Minnesota, and Fargo, North Dakota. The government wouldn't build one, so he decided to do it himself. With only a wheelbarrow, a No. 2 shovel, and an old John Deere tractor, he began to single-handedly clear and grade the land for this two-hundred-mile highway.

At the time of the news report, he was seventy-eight years old and had been working on the project for twenty years. He had finished nine miles. Only 191 to go! It sounds very American, very independent, very inspiring. But the road never got built. You have to ask yourself, *Do I want to be a lonely crusader, or do I want to be a rebuilder?*

It's significant that as Nehemiah asked for help, he "told them about the gracious hand of my God" that had been on him. He's teaching us to ask for help with the grace of God in view. In the grace of God, each of us knows that our life is a gift, and the work of rebuilding is a part of that gift.

In grace, you know it's not just about you, but about the grace that God wants to show in you and then through you. There is something about seeing your life as a grace-gift of God, instead of seeing your life as something you're solely responsible for, that inspires you to ask for the help that God tells us we all need.

Galatians 6:2 (NCV) reads, "By helping each other with your troubles, you truly obey the law of Christ." The law of Christ is the command to love one another. When you fail to ask for help, you are actually preventing someone from being able to obey Jesus' command to love!

To rebuild, you have to take a stand; you have to prepare for success; you have to review the problem; and then finally, and I think most importantly, you have to decide to ask for help.

Taking these initial steps starts the process of restoration. As simple as this sounds, it is important to remember that *a start is only a start*. Beware of the tendency to feel that this first step gets you to the finish line. The process of putting it together again will take time.

When Chad and Julie began the process of restoring their relationship, they had no idea what their journey would be like. They were soon to discover that it would take longer than expected. They saw this in the weekly dates they committed to. "It was definitely awkward at first," Julie remembered. "We made a deal to go on a date one day a week. We'd go to the park and yell and scream and fight one day a week. After a couple of those times, we were yelling less and talking more—all on swings, not even looking at each other, just swinging at the park."

Out of this painful start came a moment that let Julie know their relationship really could be restored. After a couple of months of these dates at the park, they decided to go to a restaurant. Julie had just shut down her company, and she was struggling with her identity. She wasn't sure who she was apart from running her business.

As Julie and Chad sat down at the restaurant, one of Julie's former employees spotted them and came over to their table. He asked the dreaded question, "So what are you doing now?" Julie froze. She didn't know what to say.

In her words, "I'll never forget it. Without missing a beat, Chad said, 'She's retired.' And I thought, *That's perfect; he gets me.* Before that, it was me against him, and at that moment, it was us fighting the battle together."

This was a small moment that gave them hope, a small step they could build on. It never would have happened without someone deciding to take that first step.

TAKE THE FIRST STEP:
My First Steps

DECIDE TO TAKE A STAND

As a first step, tell one other person that you are looking to begin to rebuild. Choose a person who you are confident will support and encourage you in what you are hoping to restore.

DECIDE TO PREPARE FOR SUCCESS

What one thing can you do now to prepare for what you hope God will restore?

Write down a list of the things you'll need as you begin to put something together again.

DECIDE TO REVIEW THE PROBLEM

Take some time to do a firsthand review of the problem.

Even with more internal or relational issues, it can help to go to places where the problem may have started or to days when things may have been better.

Then write a paragraph about what you see. There is something about writing down your impressions that helps you review the reality of what needs to be rebuilt.

DECIDE TO ASK FOR HELP

As a start, who could you enlist to pray for you in your process of restoration?

Chapter 3

APPRECIATE OTHERS

The words "thank you" have great power to energize your life

Though kind words do not cost much, yet they accomplish much.
Blaise Pascal

I would maintain that thanks are the highest form of thought; and that gratitude is happiness doubled by wonder.
G. K. Chesterton

How we thank God for you! Because of you we have great joy as we enter God's presence.
1 Thessalonians 3:9 NLT

D avid Maddox learned through painful experience what it takes to build a business and then rebuild that business.

David and his wife, Dorothy, moved to California during the building boom of the 1950s. What better place to be if you're a builder! It was a real wild wild West in those years. With banks almost always unavailable or unwilling to participate in a new project, builders simply put an ad in the newspaper to see if someone would answer, loan them money, and become a partner in the venture. David did a lot of building and began to gain a good reputation with his growing business.

Then he became involved in a large project that almost took his business down. The actual building went well, but unforeseen delays and problems with payments due him caused the company to be drained of all its cash. He was right back where he had started, with nothing to show for all his hard work. In a moment of discouragement, he told Dorothy, "I could have gotten a much easier job for a few hundred dollars a week, and we'd be way ahead of where we are now."

Dorothy invited David to play a round of golf with her on a nine-hole course near their home. She knew he needed some time to think, and she figured that taking out his frustration by driving a few golf balls wouldn't hurt either. As they played through that course, he worked through his frustration.

Dorothy didn't have to say much. David knew from the look in her eyes that she still believed in him. He remembered that God had made him a builder, and that although he didn't have the resources he wished he had, he did have enough to move ahead.

They decided that day to keep building, and they began to see the business turn around. Though things progressed slowly, with time and patience the business grew. There are many ways to build a business. What is special about their story is how they turned the appreciation of their assets into appreciation for God and appreciation toward others.

David had grown up in Brazil as a son of missionary parents. His brother, Paul, would become involved in ministry as an important part of Billy Graham's early team. Although he was called to a life in business, David's ministry was no less significant.

In their gratitude for what God had given, David and Dorothy generously began to bless people and churches all over the world. Many of the greatest Christian leaders of a generation past were encouraged and supported by their faith in giving. Although Dorothy has now been in heaven for many years, David continues in this work of faithfully encouraging and strengthening God's people.

This ministry was also expressed in personal ways to those David was in direct contact with in his business. In his office he has what he came to call "the desk stained with tears." Over the years, many of those he worked with came into his office to tell him through their tears that they were facing deep financial burdens. In his compassion, David often found a way to help them get back on their feet. The rebuilding of his own business allowed him to minister to many others when they needed to rebuild.

Where did David find the strength to rebuild his business when it seemed that all his work had been for nothing? What gives a person the energy to keep going when they want to give up? It's one thing to want to rebuild; it's quite another to get involved in the work of rebuilding *every day of your life*. That takes daily energy.

The place to get this energy is surprising in its simplicity. The words "thank you" hold tremendous potential for reenergizing your life.

God devotes an entire chapter of his eternal Word to Nehemiah's appreciation for those who helped rebuild the wall. We sometimes look at Nehemiah 3 as an easy chapter to skip in our reading because it's filled with a bunch of hard-to-pronounce names. God doesn't waste words, and this chapter is one example among many in the Bible of the importance of saying thank you.

We see other examples: Exodus 37 in the building of the tabernacle, 1 Kings 7 in the building of the temple, Ezra 8 in the rebuilding of the temple, and Romans 16 (as at the end of many of Paul's letters) in the building of the church.

Appreciation is the third key to putting it together again that we learn from Nehemiah. The real value of appreciation is in its result. Appreciation equals encouragement. We cannot rebuild without encouragement. We cannot do anything meaningful in life without encouragement!

Saying thank you results in encouragement both for the person who receives thanks and for the one who says thanks. The encouragement that flows from simple appreciation is one of the keys to the continued energy we need to be able to rebuild.

One of the traps we can fall into when we need to rebuild is to focus just on ourselves. We're working so hard to put it together again that we don't take time to think about anyone else. As long as we're focused only on ourselves, we're not going to find the strength we need to keep going. To be healthy, we also must focus on others. One of the simplest and most powerful ways to focus on others is to take the time to appreciate them.

Appreciation says that what someone has done is needed and noticed. The word *appreciation* means "to raise something in value"—like a stock holding or a piece of real estate that is growing in value. When you take the time to say thank you, you are raising up the value of a person. That's why this list of names is worth a chapter in God's Word, and why saying thanks is worth your time each day.

I tell David Maddox's story in this chapter because he is one of the most appreciative people I know. You can't talk to him for five minutes without seeing him find some way to appreciate and encourage you. I have personally benefited from his encouragement and witnessed how he gained energy for what he has built and rebuilt through the choice to appreciate the people around him.

He has a unique way of making his appreciation very practical. When David goes on a trip to encourage believers around the world, he always takes an extra suitcase with him—a suitcase filled with one-pound boxes of See's Candies.

While involved in more extensive projects of care for the hurting as he goes to Brazil or India, he is also taking time to appreciate the people he meets along the way: a box of candy and a thank you to a flight attendant, a porter, a taxi driver, a cook, and a custodian. These simple expressions of thanks sweeten David's spirit as much as anyone who receives the thanks.

I asked him where the practice of giving boxes of candy originated, not knowing the deeply emotional answer that would come. The habit began when his wife, Dorothy, was on the oncology floor at the UCLA Medical Center, fighting a cancer that would end up taking her life.

As David spent his hours in the hospital with her during those heartrending days, he noticed how wonderfully everyone was taking care of his wife. "Though I had the pain," he said, "I wanted them to know I appreciated what they were doing for Dorothy." So he gathered some boxes of candy and began to hand them out as a personal way of expressing his thanks.

With the loss of his wife, David was now facing the reality of rebuilding something much greater than a business. He would now need to live and serve without Dorothy after a marriage of forty-five years.

He began that process with simple expressions of appreciation. Appreciation enables us to see past our pain to the needs of others and empowers us to see past our successes to the importance of others.

Being able to thank others, even when in pain, is a quality I aspire to. I'm certainly not there yet. David started learning how to express thanks as a child of missionary parents. *Obrigado,* "thank you" in Portuguese, was a theme of his home. Most of us did not have that benefit. So where do we get started?

Nehemiah 3 gives practical insights for how to begin to say thank you to the people we work with, the family we live with, and the believers we serve with. It shows us how to develop the skill of saying thank you by being specific, sensitive, and searching.

BE SPECIFIC IN YOUR APPRECIATION

The first thing Nehemiah teaches us about being specific is *there is great power in using people's names.* Instead of saying, "Hey, guys, great job," say, "John, great job!" "Susan, that was awesome!" "Joe, unbelievable!" "Jan, wow!"

Just look at the list of names in chapter 3—the people Nehemiah calls out as those who helped rebuild the wall. I'm going to list them here, and you're going to be tempted to skip over them and move on to the next section. But if you had been involved in the project, you would read every name to see if yours is mentioned!

Eliashib

priests

men of Jericho

Zakkur

sons of Hassenaah

Meremoth

Meshullam son of Berekiah

Zadok

men of Tekoa

Joiada

Meshullam son of Besodeiah

Melatiah

Jadon

Uzziel

Hananiah

Rephaiah

Jedaiah

Hattush

Malkijah son of Harim

Hasshub

Shallum

Shallum's daughters

Hanun

residents of Zanoah

Malkijah son of Rekab

Shallun

Nehemiah son of Azbuk

Levites under Rehum

Hashabiah

Levites under Binnui

Ezer

Baruch

priests from surrounding

region

Benjamin

Azariah

Binnui

Palal

Pedaiah

temple servants

men of Tekoa

Zadok

Shemaiah

Hanun

Malkijah, a goldsmith

goldsmiths

merchants

For most of us, this is the Bible chapter of our nightmares. The nightmare? Going to a small group Bible study on Nehemiah where the host asks you to read chapter 3 for the group!

Let me give you some tips about what to do if you're ever asked to read a long list of names in the Bible. Read the names confidently.

No one else knows how to pronounce them either, so if you're confident, people will think, *Oh, that's how you say that name.*

You could do that, or you could be more honest and when you get to a name you don't know, just say, "Hard name." "Nehemiah and hard name and then hard name and hard name and hard name and the priest and hard name and hard name and the goldsmiths and the merchants rebuilt the wall." Everybody will laugh because they don't want to read those names either.

Forty-five different personal or group names are used in this chapter. Using a name says, "You are important." There is nothing sweeter than hearing your name attached to an appreciation. Of course there is work for us to do here—because we don't always remember all of the names. Taking the time to gather and remember the names is well worth the effort.

But what if you forget someone as you thank people by name? Never let the fact that you can't recognize everyone equally keep you from recognizing someone personally. Sometimes we don't use a name because we think we might leave somebody out. Nehemiah didn't worry about that.

Look at Nehemiah 3:31–32: "Next to him, Malkijah, one of the goldsmiths, made repairs as far as the house of the temple servants and the merchants . . . and between the room above the corner and the Sheep Gate the goldsmiths and merchants made repairs."

Nehemiah singled out one goldsmith as he noted that they all made repairs. The others could have felt jealous that Malkijah was highlighted. Or they could have rejoiced that one of their own was appreciated. That was their choice. But our choice needs to be to use people's names when we say thank you.

What are the names of people you're grateful for? The place to begin to appreciate them is to bring them to mind right now in God's presence. Tell God you're grateful as you say their name in prayer.

A second way to specifically give thanks is to focus on the *details of what someone has done*. Look at the details in this chapter! Nehemiah talks about walls and gates and beams and towers and bolts and bars. He's recognizing each part of what the rebuilders accomplished as they built.

Mentioning a name says, "You are important"; mentioning a detail says, "What you did was important." Nothing becomes dynamic until it becomes specific. When it becomes specific, it has greater power.

There is little power in saying, "Thanks, everyone; great job!"; there is great power in saying, "Joe, thank you for showing up early to make sure all the tables and chairs were in place for this meeting. We had a better meeting because of what you did. We all appreciate you, Joe."

When you take the time to give specific thanks, the research shows that it gives you a new energy for life. A Harvard Health article notes just a few of the studies that almost universally point to the power of gratitude:

Two psychologists, Dr. Robert A. Emmons of the University of California, Davis, and Dr. Michael E. McCullough of the University of Miami, have done much of the research on gratitude. In one study, they asked all participants to write a few sentences each week, focusing on particular topics.[1]

One group wrote about things they were grateful for that had occurred during the week. A second group wrote about daily

---

1. Robert A. Emmons and Michael E. McCullough, "Counting Blessings versus Burdens: An Experimental Investigation of Gratitude and Subject Well-Being in Daily Life," *Journal of Personality and Social Psychology* 84.2 (February 2003): 377–89, https://greatergood.berkeley.edu/pdfs/GratitudePDFs/6Emmons-BlessingsBurdens .pdf (accessed July 6, 2017).

irritations or things that had displeased them, and the third wrote about events that had affected them (with no emphasis on them being positive or negative). After 10 weeks, those who wrote about gratitude were more optimistic and felt better about their lives. Surprisingly, they also exercised more and had fewer visits to physicians than those who focused on sources of aggravation.

Another leading researcher in this field, Dr. Martin E. P. Seligman, a psychologist at the University of Pennsylvania, tested the impact of various positive psychology interventions on 411 people, each compared with a control assignment of writing about early memories.[2] When their week's assignment was to write and personally deliver a letter of gratitude to someone who had never been properly thanked for his or her kindness, participants immediately exhibited a huge increase in happiness scores. This impact was greater than that from any other intervention, with benefits lasting for a month.[3]

Suppose your doctor told you a new pill had been discovered that would give you greater happiness and energy. This pill had zero negative side effects and would cost you nothing. You'd ask the doctor to write out a prescription as fast as possible.

That's the power of gratitude, except you don't need a prescription or a trip to the drugstore! Take a moment right now to say thanks to the person whose name came to mind a moment ago. Include some detail as you thank them in a call, note, text, or email.

---

2. Martin E. P. Seligman et al., "Positive Psychology Progress: Empirical Validation of Interventions," *American Psychologist* 60 (July/August 2005): 410–21, https://greatergood.berkeley.edu/images/application_uploads/Seligman-PosPsychProgress.pdf (accessed July 6, 2017).

3. Entire extract taken from Harvard Mental Health Letter, "In Praise of Gratitude," *Harvard Health Publications*, November 2011, www.health.harvard.edu/newsletter_article/in-praise-of-gratitude (accessed July 6, 2017).

BE SENSITIVE IN YOUR APPRECIATION

Being sensitive in giving thanks means looking past the surface of the action. When we can include a comment about the motivation behind what was done, we are being sensitive. When we can take note of the significant role of the person who did it, we are taking appreciation to the next level. There are four ways to be more sensitive in saying thanks that we see modeled in Nehemiah.

Recognize the Heart behind the Action

First, *recognize the heart behind the action.* Nehemiah said, "So we rebuilt the wall till all of it reached half its height, for the people worked with all their heart" (Nehemiah 4:6). As he saw the heart behind what they had done together, Nehemiah specifically noted the heart of two men, beginning with Eliashib. "Eliashib the high priest and his fellow priests went to work and rebuilt the Sheep Gate. They dedicated it and set its doors in place, building as far as the Tower of the Hundred, which they dedicated, and as far as the Tower of Hananel" (Nehemiah 3:1).

What is this about building a gate and then putting doors on it? At first reading, this sounds very confusing. We think of a gate like a garden gate that swings on hinges. In that day, *gate* was a term that referred to the entire entry courtyards of a city. The gate of the city was an outdoor patio with divided areas where people would conduct business. So the gate had a door.

Nehemiah sees the heart behind the action when he says that Eliashib and his fellow priests not only built the gate but also dedicated it as they built it. That's the kind of appreciation that lets someone know how deeply grateful you are for them. You recognize the heart when you see a person's purpose. You recognize the heart when you state not just what someone did but also why they did it.

It's saying to a group of volunteers at a hospital, "I know you did this because you really care for the patients and their families." It's saying to a police officer, "I appreciate your heart for keeping us safe in our community." It's saying to a group of parents at a child dedication, "We all know you are dedicating your child because you want to see them grow up knowing Jesus Christ, because you have a heart for them to be close to God."

Another example of recognizing the heart behind what a person does is found in Nehemiah 3:20, where Nehemiah reports, "Next to him, Baruch son of Zabbai zealously repaired another section, from the angle to the entrance of the house of Eliashib the high priest."

Nehemiah has mentioned by name each person and the section of the wall they repaired. When he gets to Baruch, he says he "zealously repaired." In your mind's eye, try to picture somebody zealously repairing something. That was Baruch—he was putting his all into repairing that wall. You recognize the heart when you note a person's character. Nehemiah recognized a character of zeal in the way Baruch lifted and placed the stones.

You'll often see people's character in the little things. For instance, you can see a person's character in the way they drive a car. That's an "uh-oh" for many of us! Let's stay on the positive side and say you can see a person's thoughtfulness and care for others in the way they drive.

You can see character even in the way someone eats popcorn. Some people carefully eat popcorn, one kernel at a time. Others zealously eat popcorn—handfuls of popcorn with kernels flying everywhere.

When you take the time to see a person's character as you thank them, it shows that you've gone past the surface to see the heart.

Jesus did this. Jesus saw the heart when he recognized a little child's humility (Matthew 18), a poor widow's generosity (Luke 21), and a rebuffed woman's worship (John 12). He looked past the action to see the heart and thus teaches us to be sensitive as we give thanks.

Recognize Those Who Put In Extra Effort

A second way to be sensitive in your appreciation of others is to *recognize those who do more of the work.* Nehemiah writes, "Meremoth son of Uriah, the son of Hakkoz, repaired the next section" (Nehemiah 3:4). Then in verse 21, he writes, "Next to him, Meremoth son of Uriah, the son of Hakkoz, repaired another section, from the entrance of Eliashib's house to the end of it."

This is one of a number of examples of people who repaired more than one section. Nehemiah takes the time to mention all of them twice in his report. Those who go the second mile deserve a second mention. He wasn't afraid other people might be jealous of the special recognition. They gave extra effort, so he gave an extra thank you.

Single Out Leaders for Special Recognition

A third way to be sensitive in the giving of thanks is to *give recognition to the leaders.* Nehemiah mentions leader after leader. Leaders are the ones who must solve the problems and face the criticism, so they're very much in need of thanks. No one has been leading so long that they are not energized by words of appreciation. They may not do it for the appreciation, but they are certainly strengthened by it.

Leaders are important because of their influence on other people. When you say thank you to a leader, your encouragement multiplies to many others. Leaders are important because of their visibility. When you thank a leader, you are recognizing their entire team. A wise leader will take that appreciation and quickly pass it on to the people they're leading.

As a pastor and leader for many years, I can easily see how important appreciation is to me. I don't serve for the appreciation, but I honestly don't think I could serve nearly as well apart from it. We're made to need the encouragement that comes from this appreciation of others. This is why 1 Thessalonians 5:12 (NCV) reminds us, "Now, brothers and sisters, we ask you to appreciate those who work hard among you, who lead you in the Lord and teach you."

Yes, our need for encouragement can too quickly slip into an obsessive need for notice. But the fact that we sometimes struggle should not cause us to miss the importance of the encouragement that needs to be given.

Appreciation has the power to remind leaders of what's important. A number of years ago, Saddleback Church's members wrote brief notes of appreciation to Chaundel and me on the occasion of one of the anniversaries of our being with the church. As a teacher, I would have loved specific appreciations about some point I had made in one of my messages—even better, if they could have quoted it perfectly and remembered the date it was taught!

The notes we received did not talk about messages, but about unscripted moments in which we had run into someone at church or in the community—about us being among the first people they had met at church or about a word of encouragement we had been able to share. More than anything, the appreciations were for brief words of prayer on the church patio for hurts they were facing.

Reading these appreciations was a powerful reminder for those many times when I might feel too tired or too busy to spend time with people on our patio. Their appreciation guided me into what's truly important.

Offer Words of Correction When Necessary

A final way to be sensitive in expressing appreciation is to *offer words of correction when necessary*. Nehemiah writes, "The next section was repaired by the men of Tekoa, but their nobles would not put their shoulders to the work under their supervisors" (Nehemiah 3:5). As Nehemiah mentions those he appreciates, he also takes time to note those who didn't do any of the work.

Honest correction can add real power to your appreciation, because people then realize you're not just saying thanks to anyone and everyone so you can all have a feeling-positive experience. Our expressions of thanks are shown to be more genuine when we recognize that some are missing out on the blessing because they haven't joined in the effort.

Those words of correction need to be kept in balance! Nehemiah didn't make the mistake of spending the whole chapter talking to the people who didn't work. He focused on the positive giving of thanks, but he wasn't afraid to take a moment to give a word of correction. There is one verse of correction in this entire chapter of appreciation, which is a pretty good indication of the right balance.

———

When you give thanks for others specifically and sensitively, you're doing some of the most important work in rebuilding. The words of thanks you give have power to strengthen people for continued growth. Stop for a moment and give specific thanks for someone right now.

Father, help me to express sensitive thanks to others. Remind me of the character behind someone's action. Remind me of a leader who's made a difference. Remind me of someone who's gone the second mile. I give you thanks for them right now, and I ask you to show me an opportunity to pass that thanks along to them in some way today. In Jesus' name. Amen.

BE SEARCHING IN YOUR APPRECIATION

It's one thing to talk about giving thanks for others; it's quite another thing to actually do it. It's all too easy to forget. Too often, we focus more on the fact that we're not being appreciated than on how we can appreciate others. We need some practical ideas for remembering to say thank you.

As we read Nehemiah 3, we see that one of the ways Nehemiah remembered to thank everyone was by using a simple system. We can see it in verses 17–18: "Next to him, the repairs were made by the Levites under Rehum son of Bani. Beside him, Hashabiah, ruler of half the district of Keilah, carried out repairs for his district. Next to him, the repairs were made by their fellow Levites under Binnui." "Next to him . . . beside him . . . next to him"—Nehemiah remembered by going around the wall.

To become an expert at expressing thanks, you need a way to think about your thanks, to prompt your appreciation. The next few paragraphs contain some ideas about systems that can aid your memory.

Some people use the *days of the week*. For instance, they focus on their family on Monday, those they go to church with on Tuesday, people around the world on Wednesday, people they work with on Thursday, and government leaders on Friday.

If you are more space oriented in your thinking, use *the rooms of your house or the places you go* during the day. When you walk through the living room, give thanks for your family; when you go into the kitchen, give thanks for other believers; when you leave the house, give thanks for your neighbors. You can also use certain streets you drive by or subway stops to remind you to give thanks for specific groups of people.

If you are schedule focused, use your *weekly planner*. In each day's schedule write a specific group of people to show appreciation toward. Or you might put on your to-do list five people to specifically communicate your appreciation to this week. You might start with just one if you've never done this before. One is better than none!

It helps a lot of people in this system of giving thanks to use *special occasions* like birthdays and anniversaries. Instead of just signing your name in a card, take an extra moment to say a specific word of appreciation. How often have you received a card with just a signed name? We don't know what to write on a card, so we pay Hallmark to do it for us. Instead, spend a few minutes jotting down appreciation for a specific action or character quality: "I'm thankful you helped me through a tough time last year." "I'm thankful you are a kind person." "I'm thankful you have a character marked by integrity." Just one short sentence can make all the difference.

These systems help many people, and they may help you. There are two even more powerful ways to motivate yourself to say thank you: first, *appreciate others when you're being appreciated*, and second, *appreciate others when you're feeling unappreciated*. These are the two most powerful ways to motivate yourself to say thank you.

When you're being appreciated, look for someone else to

appreciate. Don't just take it in; pass it on. I'm not talking about deflecting the thanks by saying you don't deserve it, as if the person thanking you has made some kind of mistake. Instead, receive it with gratitude, and then give it to someone else.

Even more motivating is saying thank you when you're feeling unappreciated. If you're feeling that no one is noticing what you are doing, there's someone else who feels the same way. So instead of focusing on the thanks you're not getting, start to look for the person who needs the appreciation you feel you've missed out on.

Because all of us feel underappreciated at times, this one action is a complete game changer. If our feelings of not being appreciated cause us to turn inward, pretty soon no one will be giving thanks. But if they cause us to turn toward others, words of thanks and appreciation will multiply exponentially. So instead of dwelling on how unappreciated you are, encourage yourself and the other person by saying thank you to them.

THANKING GOD

In a chapter about thanking people, we cannot forget that the most important person we give thanks to is God. Let's take some time to thank the most important Person in our lives. In these principles for thanking people, you can see some wonderful truths about how to thank God.

Nehemiah taught us to use names. So when you thank God, *use his name*. Jesus taught us to pray, saying, "Our Father in heaven" (Matthew 6:9). As you use the name *Father*, you are thanking God that he is the caring Creator. The Bible gives many names for God that you can use when giving thanks. Here are just a few:

- *Jehovah Shammah* means "the LORD is there"—God is present with you. Thank him that he is present in every circumstance.
- *Jehovah Rohi* means "the LORD my shepherd"—God is your good shepherd. Thank him that he cares for you and guides you.
- *Jehovah Shalom* means "the LORD is peace"—God is your peace. Thank him for the inner calm and confidence he gives.
- *Jehovah Jireh* means "the LORD will provide"—God is your provider. Thank him for the way he meets your needs.

Nehemiah also taught us to talk about the details as we give thanks. *Take time to delight in the details* as you praise God. Psalms 103–105 provide great examples of how to do this. In these psalms, we learn how to talk to God about the details of our health and to thank him for the healing he gives. We also see how to give thanks for God's provision of details—like air to breathe and the sun in the sky. When was the last time you thanked God for the sun? When was the last time you thanked God for enough air to breathe? When you start thanking God for the details, there is an endless supply of things for which you can give thanks.

We learned from Nehemiah also to talk about a person's heart as we express thanks. As you express appreciation to God, don't just talk about what he's done for you; thank God for his character: "God, thank you that you are the God of peace." "Thank you for the wonderful beauty you create." "God, your power is way beyond what I could ever imagine." "Thank you for being such a caring and loving God." Taking time to *thank God for who he is apart from what he's done* is a very spiritually healthy thing to do.

Finally, Nehemiah modeled for us the idea of using a system to remember to say thank you. It helps many people to have a trigger that reminds them to praise God. Some use a special coin they put in their pocket or purse; others use a wristband of some sort. For many years, I've encouraged people to set an alarm on their phone based on their date of birth as a prompt to praise God. If you were born on January 23, you set an alarm for 1:23. You *could* set it for 1:23 a.m. if you're incredibly spiritual! But right after lunch at 1:23 p.m. would work better for most of us. When you hear the alarm go off, it reminds you to take just a moment to thank God.

As we come to the end of the chapter, let me remind you that you will not have the energy you need to put it together again apart from the encouragement that flows from your thanks to others and to God. Ungrateful people stay stuck where they are; grateful people move on into God's blessings. It's just that simple.

Take a few moments before moving on to the next chapter to once again give thanks to God:

Father, I thank you. Thank you for who you are—the awesome God, the almighty God, the God above all, and the God I can trust in every circumstance. Thank you for what you've done—the provision and peace and care and guidance and love that you show every day. Before I thank anybody else, I thank you. Out of my thanks to you I pray for the grace to show appreciation to those around me. In Jesus' name, I thank you. Amen.

APPRECIATE OTHERS:
My First Steps

BE SPECIFIC IN YOUR APPRECIATION

Who specifically do you need to appreciate, and what specifically do you need to appreciate them for?

BE SENSITIVE IN YOUR APPRECIATION

How can you express your appreciation more strongly by seeing the heart in what someone has done or by recognizing the extra effort they've given?

Is there a leader you need to express appreciation toward?

BE SEARCHING IN YOUR APPRECIATION

What plan will you set up to make appreciation a regular part of your life?

Pick up the phone right now or write a note—before you do anything else—to express your appreciation to someone.

Chapter 4

EXPECT AND REJECT OPPOSITION

Four common weapons of opposition and four proven steps to victory

The mind is the devil's favorite avenue of attack.
Billy Graham

To be obsessed by God is to have an effective barricade against all the assaults of the enemy.
Oswald Chambers

Fight the good fight of the faith.
1 Timothy 6:12

E ric Munyemana didn't know at age nineteen as he was driving to school with his father that he was about to become part of the rare opportunity to rebuild an entire country. Eric and his family were living in Burundi among thousands of Rwandans of the Tutsi tribe who had been in exile for decades. A policy by the government of Rwanda opened the door for the systematic discrimination and killing of those of Tutsi ethnicity.

Eric heard on the car radio a news report that an offensive had begun against those who were attacking and killing those of his tribe who remained in Rwanda. These attacks would tragically grow into the 1994 genocide against the Tutsi of Rwanda. It was a period of a hundred days in which nearly one million Rwandans lost their lives.

Eric lived in relative comfort in Burundi. His family had resources, and he could go to college and look forward to a career. But he could not get this news report out of his mind. He convinced two cousins to join him, and so their parents wouldn't plead with them not to go, they sold all they had to buy plane tickets to join the fighting as soon as possible.

Eric and his cousins left Burundi to join the Rwandan Patriotic Front in November 1990 in a war that would continue until July 1994, when the genocide stopped.

In the decades since then, Eric has been involved in the rebuilding of Rwanda through his work in business and then the church.

I've made numerous trips to Rwanda since 2004—our daughter,

Alyssa, lived there for almost three years helping churches—and have seen huge gains in the rebuilding. The changes in the infrastructure of the country are dramatically evident with every visit. The strengthening of churches, businesses, government, and families is even more striking.

Yet opposition occurred all along the way. Even after the military battles were over, the attacks continued in different forms. Whenever you are rebuilding, there will be opposition.

Sometimes, as it was in Rwanda, it is obvious that there will be a battle before victory. More often, we are shocked that not everyone is cheering us on in our striving toward such a good goal as restoring a marriage or a business. Even more shocking is the *internal* conflict of fighting ourselves against a positive change.

Because it can surprise us, perhaps it would be good to take a moment to look honestly at why there is opposition. We have opposition in doing the good work of rebuilding because we live in an evil world. We don't need a thousand-word essay on the reality of evil to know this is true. Reading the daily news gives all the evidence we need.

The opposition to the good work of rebuilding grows out of this evil. Sometimes the battle is within us; other times it comes from outside us. Our resistance to starting again may stem from deep wounds that brought insecurity. Our friends' negativity toward our efforts may come from feelings of guilt about something they didn't work to restore. In any case, the root of the problem is evil.

Whatever we want to build, there are people who want to tear it down. *Why?*

One reason is simply because it's easier. It's easier to be a critic than to act. It's easier to tear something down than to build something up.

As we rebuilt our home after a flood, it was a lot easier to tear out the waterlogged wallboard than to put the new wallboard on.

We would give people who came to help a sledgehammer and tell them to go into a room and tear out all the wallboard. They had so much fun that we'd hear them whooping it up.

When we walked into the room, they suddenly had to look sad again because it was our house that had been destroyed. But after we left the room, we soon heard the cries of excitement start up again. I understood their enjoyment. It's fun to tear things down. It's fun for a moment, but you're not building anything. People who tear down do it because it's fun for them, because it makes them feel like they're doing something.

Action always attracts critics. The famous preacher Harry Ironside used to say, "Wherever there's light, there's bugs."[1] People who bug you.

Nehemiah provides some of the best advice you'll find anywhere on how to handle opposition. We see in Nehemiah's experience four major weapons of opposition that come against us when we're working to do something good, and four ways to defuse those weapons. This is the opposition you must be ready for as you rebuild.

RIDICULE

The first weapon of those who want to tear you down is *ridicule*. Look at Nehemiah 4:1–3:

> When Sanballat heard that we were rebuilding the wall,
> he became angry and was greatly incensed. He ridiculed the
> Jews, and in the presence of his associates and the army of

---

1. Quoted in Chuck Swindoll, *Laugh Again* (Nashville: Nelson, 1995), 180.

Samaria, he said, "What are those feeble Jews doing? Will they restore their wall? Will they offer sacrifices? Will they finish in a day? Can they bring the stones back to life from those heaps of rubble—burned as they are?"

Tobiah the Ammonite, who was at his side, said, "What they are building—even a fox climbing up on it would break down their wall of stones!"

Sanballat and Tobiah were the opposition. They were leaders in the land before Nehemiah arrived. If Nehemiah were allowed to rebuild the wall, Sanballat and Tobiah would lose their power because the city would have new strength. So they started a campaign of opposition, beginning with words of ridicule.

When you want to rebuild, jokes and laughter are primary weapons in the arsenal of opponents. These effective weapons often form the first wave of attack. You tell people you want to reenergize your career, and they find it an easy target for attack. They would call it humor, but it is ridicule. It's found in phrases such as, "Like *that'll* happen," or "*What* career, flipping hamburgers?"

There is a huge difference between genuine laughter and ridicule. Genuine laughter can pull us up; ridicule puts us down. Laughter helps us relax; ridicule makes us want to quit. Laughter is a healer; ridicule is a weapon. Laughter is with us; ridicule is against us.

Ridicule comes from having the wrong perspective. Notice that Sanballat and Tobiah called it *the Jews'* wall, not God's wall. They were looking at things from a merely human perspective. They saw the wall as simply Nehemiah's bad idea that was going to negatively affect their lives. Human perspective will always ridicule steps of faith. Because faith can't happen from a human perspective, it's one of the easiest things to ridicule.

Rebuilders must have thick skin because they're going to face attack. That attack may come from an individual, but it can also come from within. One of the names for Satan in the Bible is "the accuser" (Revelation 12:10). He loves to ridicule your faith. So he'll send a thought when you want to renew your faith, a relationship, a ministry, or a dream.

Satan is not creative. With him, it's almost always the same thought: *Who do you think you are? You've failed so often, not followed through, been disappointed in relationships. Who do you think you are that you could have the kind of faith that could change anything?*

Nehemiah teaches us that to defuse the weapon of ridicule, you must choose to *redirect your thoughts*. If you focus on the ridicule, you're going to be drawn into it like falling into a deep well. Instead, you redirect your thoughts. The key to this is prayer—getting your thoughts off the enemy and back on God by talking to God about it.

Don't think that talking to God must start with some deeply spiritual expression of love and wisdom. Nehemiah begins by telling God what happened and how he feels about it:

> Hear us, our God, for we are despised. Turn their insults back on their own heads. Give them over as plunder in a land of captivity. Do not cover up their guilt or blot out their sins from your sight, for they have thrown insults in the face of the builders.
>
> So we rebuilt the wall till all of it reached its height, for the people worked with all their heart.
>
> **Nehemiah 4:4–6**

One of the most refreshing discoveries about prayer is that you don't have to have it all figured out before you talk to God. The prayer that redirects your thoughts begins by telling God where you are right now—including expressions of anger and disappointment. When we tell God what we're feeling, he's able to redirect our thinking. The psalms are absolutely filled with these kinds of prayers.

When we hide our feelings behind a veil of spiritual-sounding phrases, we end the prayer in the same place we began. Of course, God always knows what we're feeling, yet it is our expression of those feelings to him that leads us to begin to gain his perspective.

Through his prayer, Nehemiah decides to redirect his thoughts and look at the ridicule from God's perspective. Apart from God's perspective, even in seeming victories, we are still focused on proving wrong those who have ridiculed us—which is a losing strategy, because our focus has moved from God to people.

In prayer, God often works to redirect your thoughts in two very important ways.

First, you are reminded that *God's will includes opposition.* Think of a time when you started to do something good and began to experience opposition. It's easy to start to feel, *Why me, God?* You were just trying to do the right thing. Why should you have to face this?

In prayer, we begin to look beyond ourselves and realize we are not the only ones who have faced opposition. In fact, the Bible tells us we will certainly face opposition for our faith: "In fact, everyone who wants to live a godly life in Christ Jesus will be persecuted" (2 Timothy 3:12).

Jesus faced opposition, so of course we will face opposition. Prayer opens our hearts to these truths. God's will includes opposition, and God's will cannot be stopped because a few people are critical of the plan. In prayer, we redirect our thoughts from *Why me, Lord?* to *You are with me, Lord.*

Second, prayer helps you *recognize the destructiveness of retaliation*. The human response to criticism is often retaliation. In prayer, you can decide to let God fight those battles. Satan would love nothing more than to distract you from the rebuilding you need to do by getting you caught up in a battle that is not a part of the victory. Retaliation is a battle that leads to defeat every single time.

The emotional reaction to criticism is anger. We don't get to choose our emotions. If we are ridiculed, we will usually feel anger. We do get to choose what we do with our emotions. If in that anger we start to focus on proving them wrong rather than on doing what is right, we'll find ourselves drained of the time and energy we need for rebuilding.

Take your anger and express it to God and let it go. Retaliation will always lead to defeat; letting it go in God's presence is what leads to victory. You may need to pray right now:

> *God, I want my thoughts to be firmly focused on you. Instead of running that criticism through my mind again and again, I bring it to you, and I let it go. I don't want to get caught up in proving somebody else wrong. I want to get caught up in living the life you have for me. In Jesus' name. Amen.*

ATTACK

The second kind of opposition you will face is *direct attack*. Attack is when someone takes an action to prevent you from rebuilding. When sarcasm and ridicule won't work, the opposition often moves to direct attack. This attack comes when it becomes obvious that you have a chance at success. The very success that energizes and encourages you is a source of threat and fear to those who don't want you to succeed.

In Nehemiah 4:7–8, we read, "But when Sanballat, Tobiah, the Arabs, the Ammonites and the people of Ashdod heard that the repairs to Jerusalem's walls had gone ahead and that the gaps were being closed, they were very angry. They all plotted together to come and fight against Jerusalem and stir up trouble against it."

The attack against Nehemiah is a reminder of two truths about opposition.

First, *people ridicule a vision, but they try to destroy a reality.* Once a vision becomes a reality, the only way to defeat it is to destroy it. So when you set out to change the culture of a church to be more focused on the lost in the community, those who don't want the church to change will snicker at you over Sunday dinner. But when you actually begin to reach enough people to change the church, they'll try to remove you from leadership. Of course, they won't say it's because you're reaching people for Christ—that would sound foolish. They'll find something else about you or your family to attack, pretending that *that* is the real issue.

The second truth is that *initial success doesn't silence opposition; it intensifies it.* We all have this hope that those who criticize us will see that we were right when success begins to happen. We dream of them knocking on our office door and saying, "I have to admit it; you were right all along." This does happen, but all too rarely. More often, the fact that our plan for the company is proving to be the right one will cause those who disagreed to feel more threatened and to intensify their attack.

What do you do when someone is making trouble for you by trying to tear down what you're building? You can't just pretend the attack isn't there. It *is* an attack, and it has the power to destroy. When you face attack, the strategy for success is to *reposition your forces*. We learn this from Nehemiah in 4:9: "But we prayed to our God and we posted a guard day and night to meet this threat."

Nehemiah took some of the wall builders and turned them into guards. He repositioned his forces by taking the resources God had given him and putting some of them to work in defeating the opposition.

He had to make some changes for that to happen. To defeat the opposition, we will often have to make some changes. Many times, we settle for defeat and wonder why God won't allow us to move ahead, simply because we haven't considered the possibility of making a change.

I remember many years ago, a family we were close to from a former church called us and said, "We're having a struggle with our daughter, and we're wondering if she could live with you for the summer. We need to make a change so she doesn't keep going down the road she's on." She came to live with us, and to her credit, she began to see the truth of where she was headed and made a huge change in the direction of her life. To get a different perspective, she needed to do something different.

If your business is under attack, what changes do you need to make? Maybe you need to reposition some of your staff to positively answer this challenge. If you're under attack spiritually, what changes do you need to make? You may need to stay away from certain people or circumstances. Or you may need to begin spending more time in God's Word or get an accountability partner to encourage you along the way.

Notice what happens next in Nehemiah's account of the opposition to the rebuilding:

From that day on, half of my men did the work, while the other half were equipped with spears, shields, bows and armor. The officers posted themselves behind all the people of Judah who were building the wall. Those who carried materials did their work with one hand and held a weapon in the other, and each of the builders wore his sword at his side as he worked. But the man who sounded the trumpet stayed with me.

Nehemiah 4:16–18

Nehemiah didn't stop building to fight against the attack. If you do this, you'll end up spending the rest of your life fighting the attack, and you'll never get back to building. Nehemiah had learned this all-important lesson: *you build while you fight.* One of the ways your enemies keep you from building is by making sure you are totally caught up in defending yourself against the attack. When the attack comes, reposition your forces and keep building!

DISCOURAGEMENT

In Nehemiah 4:10–12, we see a third kind of opposition we all face: *discouragement.*

Meanwhile, the people in Judah said, "The strength of the laborers is giving out, and there is so much rubble that we cannot rebuild the wall."

Also our enemies said, "Before they know it or see us, we will be right there among them and will kill them and put an end to the work."

> Then the Jews who lived near them came and told us ten
> times over, "Wherever you turn, they will attack us."

The invitation to become discouraged gets louder and louder. An attitude of discouragement is contagious. If you start listening, you'll catch it too. Ridicule and attack hit at you from the outside, discouragement from the inside. Because of this, it can be a far more destructive enemy.

Beth Moore writes, "Make no mistake: Satan's specialty is psychological warfare. If he can turn us on God ('It's not fair!'), turn us on others ('It's their fault!'), or turn us on ourselves ('I'm so stupid!'), we won't turn on him. If we keep fighting within ourselves and losing our own inner battles, we'll never have the strength to stand up and fight our true enemy."[2]

One of the reasons discouragement is so invasive is found in this simple truth: you can always find a reason to be discouraged. As an imperfect person in an imperfect world, of course there are reasons you can tell yourself that any project or dream has no chance of success. In Nehemiah's case, the reasons were too little strength, too much rubble, and too many enemies.

Nehemiah 4:12 reads, "Then the Jews who lived near them came and told us ten times over, 'Wherever you turn, they will attack us.'" *Ten times over*, the people were told to be discouraged. The people who encourage you usually just tell you once; the people who want to discourage you keep saying it again and again. *Ten times over*—it seems like more than you can bear.

Maybe you're facing discouragement right now. You feel you are never going to have victory over that sin or begin to restore

---

2. Beth Moore, *Believing God* (Nashville: Broadman & Holman, 2004), 227–28.

that relationship or have a great business or ministry. Nehemiah teaches that the answer to discouragement is to *restore your confidence*. You do this by meeting discouragement head-on with a more powerful weapon. What's more powerful than discouragement? Encouragement! It'll beat discouragement every time.

Look at what happens next in Nehemiah's account:

> Therefore I stationed some of the people behind the lowest points of the wall at the exposed places, posting them by families, with their swords, spears and bows. After I looked things over, I stood up and said to the nobles, the officials and the rest of the people, "Don't be afraid of them. Remember the Lord, who is great and awesome, and fight for your families, your sons and your daughters, your wives and your homes."
>
> **Nehemiah 4:13–14**

Nehemiah chooses to encourage the people in two specific ways: through service and through worship.

First, *he encouraged them through service*. He stationed them by families to guard the walls. He got them involved in the answer to their discouragement. One of the greatest ways to attack discouragement is to look for someone to serve.

Restoring your confidence never comes by focusing on yourself. You may need to do some work within yourself with a counselor if you are in a state of depression; that's an important starting place for many of us. But in the end, the discouragement lifts only when you find yourself able to serve others again.

God made us to serve. In posting the people by families, Nehemiah got them serving together so they could encourage each other as they carried out the work. One of the keys to defeating discouragement is finding a place to serve.

The second thing Nehemiah did was to *encourage them to remember and worship the Lord*. Restoring your confidence will never come from looking at your circumstances. As we saw earlier, circumstances are not a reliable source of confidence because they're always changing.

Circumstances can't be trusted, but God *can* always be trusted. Continue to rely on him, regardless of the circumstances, as your source of confidence. As Corrie ten Boom pictured it, "When a train goes through a tunnel and it gets dark, you don't throw away your ticket and jump off. You sit still and trust the engineer."[3] Remember the Lord and worship him, for he is great and awesome. That's where your confidence is going to come from.

One of the most discouraging times in my life came as Chaundel and I waited to become parents. We had been married for six years and had been trying for some time. When we went to the doctor for tests, we were told that we would not be able to have children.

We were devastated. Being parents was one of our greatest dreams. Our financial resources were limited, and so adoption seemed out of reach for us. I can still distinctly remember times of allowing my mind to soak in the discouragement of an unfulfilled dream.

Then one day it hit me. God had put that dream into our hearts. He could take it away if he wanted to, but until he did, he could be trusted to somehow fulfill what he had put into our hearts. My mind began to turn from discouragement to worship by recognizing that I could trust God's love in every circumstance.

---

3. Corrie ten Boom, *Jesus Is Victor* (Grand Rapids: Revell, 1984), 183.

As we've walked with families through infertility over the years, we have seen God work powerfully through new life directions, infertility treatments, and adoptions. In our case, his answer was to miraculously give us one and then two and then three children. Ryan, Alyssa, and Luke give us powerful evidence that even in our discouragement, God is at work and can be trusted.

Take a moment to talk to God about your discouragement.

Lord, I don't want to live discouraged; I want to live encouraged. So I ask for your encouragement right now. I pray that you'd show me a place to serve. And even though I may not feel like it, give me the strength to serve. Lord, give me the heart to look to you, to remember you, and to worship you. You are a great and awesome God. You are a God who loves me and a God who will encourage me in anything and everything. In Jesus' name I pray. Amen.

DISTRACTION

When the opposition of ridicule, attack, or discouragement doesn't defeat us, there is a fourth strategy that quietly works against us: *distraction.* We often find ourselves fighting hard for a victory, only to allow something to distract us away from the achievement of that victory. Once we begin to experience success, Satan would love nothing better than to distract us from that success. We could talk about a hundred kinds of distraction—from the obviously bad to the seemingly good.

Nehemiah teaches us how to face the enemy of distraction: *remember your priorities.* The opposite of distraction is focus, and when you focus on what's important, the distractions tend to melt away. Nehemiah battled three major distractions we will all face.

First is the distraction of *false opportunities*. In Nehemiah 6:1–2, we read these words:

> When word came to Sanballat, Tobiah, Geshem the Arab and the rest of our enemies that I had rebuilt the wall and not a gap was left in it—though up to that time I had not set the doors in the gates—Sanballat and Geshem sent me this message: "Come, let us meet together in one of the villages on the plain of Ono."
>
> But they were scheming to harm me.

Nehemiah was tempted to be distracted by this opportunity to make everything right with his enemies. It looked like a wonderful opportunity, but it was a false promise. They were using the promise as bait to get him to a place where they could harm him. The significant lesson here is that not every promise of something good is good. Sometimes it's the distraction of a false opportunity. Nehemiah's opposition invited him to the plains of Ono, and as many preachers have noted, he wisely said no to Ono!

In 6:3, Nehemiah writes, "So I sent messengers to them with this reply: 'I am carrying on a great project and cannot go down. Why should the work stop while I leave it and go down to you?'" Nehemiah saw immediately that a meeting would be a waste of time. His project was rebuilding the wall, not engaging in political talks with these enemies. He wasn't tempted by the false promise, because he knew his priorities. He said no, and he kept saying no.

When you start to rebuild a relationship, there may well be someone who comes in with a false promise of a better relationship.

Say no! When your business starts to be successful again, someone may well distract you with the promise of a quicker payday. Say no! When you see the place of ministry where God wants you to work next, there will almost always be an offer of some place where the grass seems like it would be greener. Say no!

One of the keys to saying no to the false opportunities put in front of us is unselfishness. If we're always chasing after what would be selfishly best for our bank accounts or our egos, we'll find ourselves falling for false promises for the rest of our lives. The best protection against being distracted by false opportunities is a heart for serving God and others.

Second, Nehemiah's opponents try to distract him through *gossip*:

> Then, the fifth time, Sanballat sent his aide to me with the same message, and in his hand was an unsealed letter in which was written:
>
> "It is reported among the nations—and Geshem says it is true—that you and the Jews are plotting to revolt, and therefore you are building the wall. Moreover, according to these reports you are about to become their king and have even appointed prophets to make this proclamation about you in Jerusalem: 'There is a king in Judah!' Now this report will get back to the king; so come, let us meet together."
>
> **Nehemiah 6:5–7**

We see here some of the favorite phrases of those who gossip: "it is reported," and "this person says it's true." Gossip is a horrific sin that tears apart friendships, families, businesses, and churches. It seems like such an innocent sin, but there is a reason it is listed alongside greed, depravity, and murder in Romans 1:29. Nehemiah's enemies are trying to use gossip to distract him and to destroy what he is building. Gossipers love to destroy what others are building. It gives them a twisted sense of power.

Nehemiah avoided distraction when he faced gossip by simply telling the truth and moving on. I don't know of a better answer to a gossiper anywhere in all of literature than the answer that Nehemiah gives in 6:8: "Nothing like what you are saying is happening; you are just making it up out of your head."

You have to love this answer! It's the most refreshing comment you could ever make about gossip. You just tell the truth and then forget the rumor. That's how you deal with gossip. You don't try to answer the gossiper or defend against everything they are saying. They'll just make up more gossip. They're just trying to distract you. Satan is trying to distract you from what God is doing.

The third way the opponents try to distract Nehemiah is through *fear*: "One day I went to the house of Shemaiah son of Delaiah, the son of Mehetabel, who was shut in at his home. He said, 'Let us meet in the house of God, inside the temple, and let us close the temple doors, because men are coming to kill you—by night they are coming to kill you'" (Nehemiah 6:10). It almost sounds ridiculous when we read it now, but for Nehemiah, it was designed to create fear at the moment of victory.

We often face the inner fear that we're going to fail right before we cross the finish line. This distraction can come into your mind without anyone else having to say a word. You wonder who you think you are to be able to achieve this. You tell yourself you've failed before, and so you're going to fail this time too. You think, *What if something goes wrong now that we're almost there?* We can become our own worst enemy in this distraction of fear.

When you face the distraction of fear, you remember your priorities by recognizing God has priority over any fear, because he is greater than every fear. We learn from Nehemiah's example in 6:11–13:

> But I said, "Should a man like me run away? Or should some-one like me go into the temple to save his life? I will not go!" I realized that God had not sent him, but that he had prophe-sied against me because Tobiah and Sanballat had hired him. He had been hired to intimidate me so that I would commit a sin by doing this, and then they would give me a bad name to discredit me.

The opponents wanted to be able to say that Nehemiah was hiding in fear while asking everyone else to take the risks. They were trying to discredit him as a leader. Nehemiah kept his focus by not hiding from his fear.

If the thing you fear is real, then deal with it. If it is a sense of fear that you can't identify with any real cause, then reject it. The last thing you should do is hide from your fears. Whenever we hide from a fear, it grows stronger. When you face a fear, deal with a fear, and share a fear, it loses its power.

Nehemiah decided that his *trust in God* would determine his actions, not his fear. He knew he was not the kind of person who was going to run into the temple to save his life while everyone else risked their lives. He was the kind of person who was going to trust God in every circumstance. He started by trusting God and decid-ing to keep trusting God. By God's grace, every one of us is meant to be that kind of person.

Nehemiah trusted God through all oppositions against him,

and the outcome is recorded in 6:15–16: "So the wall was completed on the twenty-fifth of Elul, in fifty-two days. When all our enemies heard about this, all the surrounding nations were afraid and lost their self-confidence, because they realized that this work had been done with the help of our God."

Instead of losing his confidence, Nehemiah *restored* his confidence. When he restored his confidence, all his enemies lost their confidence. God wants you to experience this kind of victory in your rebuilding.

———————

As I talked with Eric Munyemana about the opposition his people faced in the rebuilding of Rwanda, I was amazed at how closely it paralleled the battles Nehemiah faced.

Their battle also began with *ridicule*. In Rwanda, the ridicule came through the media over what were known as "hate radio and TV stations." Nehemiah's enemies demeaned his people as a bunch of poor, feeble Jews. The Rwandans who were under attack were called cockroaches. Ridicule was used to make their lives seem as nothing. The battle would have been lost from the beginning if they hadn't found the courage to reject this hate speech.

That ridicule grew into *attack* as some in the majority Hutus began to take the lives of the minority Tutsis. The taking of life was rationalized by thinking of enemies as "less than human." Once the attacks began, the forces in the surrounding countries had to be *repositioned* to fight in Rwanda if a victory was to be won.

As the battle wore on, those under attack had to deal with the possibility of *discouragement*. The army was no longer fighting each day, and there were long hikes for soldiers carrying heavy burdens on their heads to get to places where they could protect the people from further attack.

Eric shared that as a young man who had grown up in comfortable surroundings, he became familiar with the challenges of lack of food, water, shower facilities, and bathrooms on a daily basis. He saw in those days the power of good leaders to encourage, even in the midst of discouraging circumstances, as they reminded the soldiers of the purpose of their fight.

Finally, in the years since the genocide, there have been many battles with *distraction*. Eric observed that in the heat of the fighting, all worked together in selfless unity. After the fighting ended, egos began to rise again—as well as an intense temptation to get trapped in anger over those whose lives had been lost.

Knowing that anger would only bring about the same cycle of hate that had caused the genocide, Rwanda made the choice as a nation to forgive. As a church leader, Eric could see how hungry people were for the message of God's forgiveness toward them and then their own forgiveness toward others. Forgiveness was their only way out, their only way forward.

One of the places this forgiveness was offered was in the local Gacaca court system of community justice. *Gacaca* means a "patch of grass" where people had historically met to settle village disputes. With more than one hundred thousand people accused of participating in the killings, it would have taken decades for the traditional court system to handle the trials.

The Gacaca courts were used to conduct the trials, primarily of those willing to confess their crimes. In these courts, regular members of the community served as lawyers and witnesses. The Gacaca judges were laypeople elected from all communities in Rwanda because of their integrity.

Perpetrators were called before the courts to explain their actions, admit their crimes, and ask for forgiveness. This process informed survivors about what happened to family members and was important for preventing a prolonged period of retribution. The aim of the courts was for both justice and, more important, reconciliation.

The tradition surrounding this court had been to drink together at the close of the discussions as a sign of reconciliation. Out of that tradition came the community offering of forgiveness to the perpetrators of genocide, even as they were being sentenced.

As I heard from Eric and personally observed over the years, this process of asking and giving forgiveness is the most important key to the rebuilding of Rwanda. Apart from forgiveness, we always get stuck in our past. Only through forgiveness are we able to look to God's purposes for our future.

Unforgiveness will always pull you away from your priorities and purposes into past shame or bitterness. You may need a personal kind of Gacaca court meeting with God right now in which you settle, or resettle, two things in your heart:

You are forgiven. If you're not certain you are forgiven, you can be certain right now. This is because forgiveness is based not on what you have done or can do, but on what Jesus did for you on the cross. Forgiveness is a gift, so it is impossible to earn it.

Pray right now:

Jesus, thank you for paying the price for the wrong things I've done by dying on the cross. I am sorry for my sins and want to live the kind of life you created me to live. I accept the gift of forgiveness that you offer me. I personalize what you say in 1 John 1:9. As I confess my sins, I can know you will forgive my sins, because I can trust you to do what is right. You will cleanse me from all the wrongs I have done.

You can forgive. Out of the grace of God's forgiveness toward you, you can find the strength to forgive others. Remember that forgiveness does not mean you won't remember what happened. It does not mean there are no consequences for the hurt that was done to you. The forgiven murderers in Rwanda were still imprisoned for their crimes. Forgiveness simply means you let it go into the hands of almighty God instead of holding on to the bitterness.

I realize I'm dealing very briefly here with the huge subject of forgiving others. You may need to read some books to work through this process of forgiveness. Lewis B. Smedes's *Forgive and Forget* is one great resource among many.[4] You forgive not for the offender's sake, but for *your* sake so hidden bitterness does not erode your ability to experience God's love.

There is a final truth about opposition we must not miss. Human determination is not enough to defeat these opponents. Victory comes from your *relationship with God.* Nehemiah exemplifies dependence on God at every point in the battle: he talks to God in prayer, follows God in the changes, listens to God in his encouragement, and lives by means of God's priorities through God's Word.

If you're trying to do this alone, of course you're feeling defeated. You'll be amazed at the difference you see when you begin to lean on God's strength instead of trying to do good things for God based on your own strength. As you rely on God's strength, when the renewal is completed, you can tell a story that will point people to the God who gave you strength.

---

4. Lewis B. Smedes, *Forgive and Forget: Healing the Hurts We Don't Deserve*, 2nd ed. (San Francisco: HarperOne, 2007).

EXPECT AND REJECT OPPOSITION:
My First Steps

ARE YOU FACING RIDICULE?

How will you *redirect your thoughts*?

Begin by honestly telling God all that you feel about the opposition you are facing.

ARE YOU FACING ATTACK?

How will you *reposition your forces*?

Start by asking yourself what changes you need to make to prepare you to face this opposition.

ARE YOU FACING DISCOURAGEMENT?

How will you *restore your confidence*?

Who in your circles can you serve, even as you are facing discouragement? Possibly someone who is also facing discouragement?

Make the choice to continue to worship with others at church as you face this discouragement.

ARE YOU FACING DISTRACTION?

How will you *remember your priorities*?

Ask yourself whether there are things distracting you from the priority of what God is putting together again. If you're especially courageous, ask some friends to share with you the distractions they see in your life.

How might false promises, gossip, or fear be distracting you?

Chapter 5

BUILD ON YOUR SUCCESSES

Success is not a pinnacle to stand on; it's a foundation to build on

The measure of our success will be the measure of our ability to help others.

F. B. Meyer

Faithfulness in little things is a big thing.

Saint John Chrysostom

David continued to succeed in everything he did, for the LORD was with him.

1 Samuel 18:14 NLT

I first met Danny Duchene when a group of pastors from Saddleback Church went to minister to prisoners in Jonestown Prison in Northern California. Danny was one of those inmates, serving a life sentence for his involvement in a double murder at the age of eighteen.

Danny didn't grow up in the gang culture of the city, but in the supposedly safe environment of the suburbs of a smaller city. Here is his story in his own words:

I grew up in Redding, California, with my mom and stepdad and five brothers. One thing I remember about my childhood is that I had a lot of freedom to do whatever I wanted to do. I was a latchkey kid, and by the fourth grade, I was spending entire summers by myself. My parents had nice homes and cars, and I grew up thinking that the goal of life was just having nice things.

Possessions became a substitute for loving relationships . . . I started partying on the weekends and discovered how easy it was to make friends because I was the one who had the car and had the freedom to throw a party while my parents were out.

Shortly after I turned sixteen, I came home from school one day, and my parents were sitting with a friend with thousands of dollars in cash spread out on the kitchen table. I was told that they were going on a business trip to Peru and that I would see them at Christmas. So I was left to take care of my eighteen-month-old little brother with the help of some family friends.

But my parents did not return from that trip. Instead on Christmas Eve 1979, I learned that my parents had been arrested in Mexico for smuggling cocaine. This was a total shock since my parents were neither drug users nor drinkers.

The news that my parents were in jail in another country filled me with fear. But soon my fear turned to anger. To cope with all the painful emotions I felt on that Christmas Day, I drove to a parking lot and got high in my car. Getting high gave me temporary relief. And I remember committing myself to a life of getting high every day.

Little did I realize that the decision to stuff my fear and anger and soothe myself with drugs would become an addiction that would imprison me long before I went to prison . . . I became more and more impulsive and began a downward spiral of one bad decision after another.

I started committing crimes to support my drug habits . . . There were people around me who loved me and tried to help, but I quickly became addicted to my way of dealing with all my loneliness and pain . . .

As my debts piled up, I struggled to keep myself supplied with an increasing need for alcohol and drugs. I was reckless and never worried about getting caught for my crimes, and I certainly didn't consider the consequences to others. I was only thinking of myself. All this came to a crisis when I was part of a crime in which two men were killed.

Thankfully, I was quickly arrested in September of 1982, which I also called being rescued. Sitting in a county jail before my trial, it took about three weeks to withdraw from the drugs and alcohol, but once I became sober, the full weight of my crimes came crashing down on my conscience.

I was overwhelmed with depression and remorse as I realized how many people I had hurt. I believed I was lost and going to hell, and I was truly, truly afraid.

It was at my lowest point that God's mercy showed up in my life. God began bringing a lot of Christians to see me who shared the love and mercy of God with me. At first, this good news seemed over my head. It seemed unbelievable and too good to be true that God loved me and wanted to show me mercy after all I had done to hurt others . . .

But the message of God's mercy eventually got through to me. I learned that Jesus could give me a fresh start, changing me from the inside out . . . I decided to open up my life to Jesus and begin to serve him with whatever kind of life I had left. And knowing my crimes, I didn't expect the rest of my life to be very long.

On November 7, 1982, in a county jail waiting my trial, I asked Jesus to forgive all my sins, come inside, and to take charge as the Lord of my life . . .

The Bible says in Romans 5:20 that "where sin increased, grace increased all the more." And I rapidly grew spiritually while in the county jail. I was hungry to know more about this God who had shown me love and mercy, and I wanted him to use me, even in prison.

Graciously God blessed me with mentors, spiritual fathers, and spiritual mothers who took the time and raised me in the Lord. At my trial, I was convicted and given a double life sentence for two deaths. And as a nineteen-year-old, I was sent to prison for life in August 1983, never expecting to see the outside world again.

But I was thankful to be in Christ, and inside I had been liberated. Let me make this clear: I never expected that I would ever be paroled—but I was free.[1]

It was striking to me that Eric Munyemana, whose story we looked at in the last chapter, and Danny were both nineteen when their lives dramatically changed. Eric heroically headed to war, and Danny tragically was sent to prison. It's a reminder that no matter what our circumstances, God is at work in our lives to put the pieces back together in a way that shows his power.

When everything seems to be coming together, look desperately to God as the only one who can truly build what is great. When everything seems to be falling apart, look desperately to God as the only one who can rebuild out of the ruins of what has been lost.

Danny began to build his life on the freedom that Christ had given him, even while in prison. He started by serving the inmates in ministry and then as a Bible teacher under the mentorship of his chaplain.

We met him after he had been in prison for twenty years because he had decided to start Purpose Driven Life groups in his prison. He dreamed of having fifty men sign up; two hundred men signed up instead! These two hundred men would form into a church, worshiping together, meeting each week in what grew to be sixty small groups, and supporting each other in their journeys to become free of their addictions in Celebrate Recovery groups.

The impact of this church within a prison was so dramatic that the warden couldn't help but notice. The fights in the prison yard leading to lockdowns dropped from a regular occurrence to rare

---

1. "Pastor Danny Duchene's Message of God's Mercy at Saddleback Church," April 2, 2016, www.youtube.com/watch?v=aVNuGvr48GQ (accessed July 6, 2017).

instances. "What have you done to my prison?" the warden asked us. News of the ministry spread, leading to the start of Purpose Driven Life and Celebrate Recovery groups in other prisons. Eventually, the story hit the front page of the *New York Times*.

I'll never forget watching Danny and his fellow leaders during our visit with this new church as they took a group of about one hundred men to the middle of the prison yard. They were there to express their intention to be a church in this place. The men took off their shoes to state that even that prison yard could be holy ground when dedicated to God. It's a risky thing to take shoes off in the yard, when there might be a need to fight or flee at any moment.

Then they turned to each of the cell blocks and boldly shouted together, "We claim Cell Block A for the purposes of God . . . We claim Cell Block B for the purposes of God." A reminder of this day hangs proudly on my wall in the form of an honorary certificate of membership in the Sierra Christian Center Purpose Driven Fellowship.

These men were not waiting to build on the grace they had been given in Jesus Christ; they started right where they were.

More than a decade later, Danny was to face one of his greatest challenges. It came in the form of an unexpected blessing. With a double life sentence, he had no hope of ever being released from prison. But based on his service to others over his entire prison term and a letter from Rick Warren stating a desire to have him work with Saddleback Church to help prisoners across the nation, Danny was given a parole.

The challenge came in what he would do with this unexpected freedom. A wise chaplain had told him how easily he could become overwhelmed with the number of decisions he would now have to make every day. In prison, what he wore, what he ate, and what his daily schedule looked like were all decided for him. He compared it to moving from a small pond to a fast-rushing river.

I asked Danny what kept him secure in this transition. He told me there were three pillars. First was the priority of his love for Christ. Instead of getting caught up in all of the new opportunities he now had, he committed to get caught up in his worship of God.

Second was his commitment to serve others. Being released from prison did not mean he was released from ministry. Far from it. The ministry to others that he had carried out in prison to build a successful life would be what he now did on the outside.

The third pillar was what he called "living my amends." While he knows he is forgiven by Christ for his crimes, he also knows that lives were devastated. He can't make amends to those whose lives were taken, but he can live his amends in the ways he gives to others. Through God's grace, he is turning from his guilt toward love and ministry.

Today, based on that heart for ministry, Danny Duchene serves on the staff of Saddleback Church as the pastor who takes Celebrate Recovery inside prison walls. He is building his life on the successful ministry he started while in prison.

THE STEWARDSHIP OF SUCCESS

One of the key questions in life has to do with what you are going to do when your greatest successes come, whether that success is personal, relational, or vocational. This is the question Danny had to face when he got his parole.

You can treat a success in one of three ways: like a trophy, a threat, or a foundation.

You can treat a success like a trophy. Put it on the shelf to admire it, and there it dies. Nothing else comes out of that success. More and more, it becomes a story from the past.

You can treat a success like a threat. More of us do this than you might think. We run from a success because we realize it's going to bring new responsibilities into our lives. Any parent who doesn't admit that sometimes they want to run away from that responsibility is not an honest parent. It can be overwhelming to think, *I've got to raise this human being.*

You can treat a success like a foundation. Instead of treating the success like a trophy or a threat, you can use it as a foundation. Successes are given for you to build on. Your greatest success is not a pinnacle to stand on; it's a foundation to build on. Your successes are one of your greatest stewardships.

Nehemiah had a great success; the rebuilding of the wall was completed. Look again at these verses that express the success: "So the wall was completed on the twenty-fifth of Elul, in fifty-two days. When all our enemies heard about this, all the surrounding nations were afraid and lost their self-confidence, because they realized that this work had been done with the help of our God" (Nehemiah 6:15–16).

Let's slow down and look closely at three things in these verses. First, notice how long it took to rebuild the wall: fifty-two days. A wall that had been in ruins for more than 140 years was rebuilt in less than two months. That's the kind of miracle God can work when you decide you want to put it together again.

We look at what we need to rebuild and feel that it's impossible because all we see is the rubble and the ruin. The rubble is a lie! If all you look at is the rubble, all you're looking at is the lie. You can never rebuild out of the rubble; you can only rebuild out of God's resources. When you get your eyes off of what you can't do and get your focus on what God can do, amazing change often happens much more quickly than you could have imagined.

Second, notice the result: the enemies lost their confidence. This was a great personal victory for Nehemiah after his battles with these enemies. It's a reminder to not listen to the seeming confidence of someone who opposes our faith. Their confidence will melt when they see what God can do.

Finally, notice the reference: chapter 6, verses 15 and 16. There are 406 verses in the book of Nehemiah—119 come before the wall is completed, and 285 come after these verses about the wall being completed. When the wall is finished, Nehemiah is less than one-third of the way through the project! He achieved his greatest success, which means he now has a lot of work to do. People needed to be appointed to care for the wall, and plans needed to be made to revitalize the city within the wall.

Nehemiah continued to rebuild because he knew what to do when the initial task was completed. His life had not become the rebuilding of the wall. He kept in focus that the wall was being built for a purpose, and he began to work toward that purpose of a place for the people of God to worship and live once the wall was rebuilt. He was able to change gears and begin to build on the success so the people of Israel could benefit from that success.

Building on success is the key to sustaining the success that God gives. So how do we do that? Many business books have been written about this, and we can learn much from them. Nehemiah showed good business sense in the decisions he made, and he did so with a blending of strategy and spiritual dependence on God that has rarely been matched. We can learn four lessons from Nehemiah for stewarding our successes.

Secure Your Investment

The first step to build on your success is to *secure that success*. Nehemiah 7:1 reads, "After the wall had been rebuilt and I had set the doors in place . . ." The wall needed doorways so people could get in and out of the city. If the builders had left the doorways without doors, all the work they had done would have been wasted.

To build the wall and not set the doors in place would have meant enemies or animals could just as easily have gotten in as if there were no walls. Doors made the walls effective for keeping out and for letting in. You secure your success by protecting your investment.

When it came to this protection of an investment, Nehemiah took personal responsibility. He personally set the doors in place. He didn't personally build the whole wall; he delegated all along, but he put up the doors.

He knew we can get to a place of great victory at the completion of a project and then not do the one final thing to secure the success. We get tired, and so we say we'll wait. There are some things that can wait, but protecting the investment of what we have rebuilt must be done immediately. Otherwise we could lose all that we've fought to restore.

In a business that you've rebuilt, this can mean hiring people to sustain what you started or getting patents to protect the investment of what you've created. In a marriage that you've done the hard work to restore, it means being humble enough to recognize how easily you could slip back into the old patterns that got your relationship in trouble. So you build in some new patterns, such as a daily walk together to keep communication fresh or a regular time away together to keep your connection strong.

This seems like such an obvious step. Why does it so often go undone? One of the reasons is that we don't prepare for the slump. With every great success, there is a slump. With every mountaintop, there is a valley. We always expect a loss of energy after a failure, but we're often surprised by the physical and mental slump that follows a success.

It is a combination of the natural letdown from the adrenaline of the success and the emotional depletion that comes from the giving of yourself. Be prepared for it. Don't let it overwhelm you, and let God carry you through. And then make it a priority to personally secure your investment when you get to the other side of the slump.

Don't Do It Alone

The second thing Nehemiah did to build on his success was to *appoint workers.* That's the decision to delegate, to not do it alone. Think of it this way: if God has given you a success, it's not just for you; he wants other people involved in what he is doing.

Nehemiah 7:1 reads, "After the wall had been rebuilt and I had set the doors in place, the gatekeepers, the musicians and the Levites were appointed." He specifically delegated people for all the jobs that had to be done now that the wall was rebuilt.

Nehemiah understood the importance of including others, so immediately after the wall was completed and the doors set in place, he appointed gatekeepers. If you have a door, you need somebody to open and shut the door. If Nehemiah hadn't appointed gatekeepers, he would have been running from gate to gate in the morning and at night, opening and shutting the doors.

He also appointed musicians and Levites, people who would help the city of Jerusalem be a place of worship. He made sure the city would fulfill the purpose for which it was made through the people he involved. One of the greatest mistakes we make in delegation is only getting help with the daily tasks. We also need people to help us with the overall purpose.

Getting others involved keeps a great success from becoming a great burden. It's easy to become overwhelmed by your successes. What started out as a great achievement will become a huge burden if you try to manage it all by yourself.

The work begins to grow beyond what you can do by yourself. On top of that, the success attracts others who want to learn from what you did right. The feeling starts to hit you—*What have I created? How will I manage it? I just want to run away and start all over again.*

Don't run away, but also don't run from that feeling. In fact, embrace that moment of feeling overwhelmed as an invitation into one of the greatest decisions you'll ever make. When you're feeling overwhelmed, remember that you're not supposed to do it all alone. God didn't create you to do it all alone. This is the feeling that says, *Who else needs to be involved?*

One of the great examples of delegation in history is found in the life of Moses. He was judging the disputes of the people of Israel and found himself overwhelmed by the needs. He was talking to people from morning to night, with the task unfinished at the end of every day.

The great success of seeing God set the people free had become for Moses the burden of a task with no end in sight. It was a sure sign of his need to delegate, and his father-in-law, Jethro, gave him the wise advice to include others in the work: "You and these people who come to you will only wear yourselves out. The work is too heavy for you; you cannot handle it alone" (Exodus 18:18). His words are a reminder that the failure to delegate is a burden not only on us, but also on all those who must now wait for us because we are too busy.

The practical advice given by Jethro was to divide the people into groups of thousands, hundreds, fifties, and tens. Then Moses was to appoint capable men of integrity as judges over them: "And let them judge the people at all times. Then it will be that every great matter they shall bring to you, but every small matter they themselves shall judge. So it will be easier for you, for they will bear the burden with you" (Exodus 18:22 NKJV).

Stop bearing the burden alone. You were not meant to bear the burden alone.

These principles of delegation apply very obviously when you are rebuilding a business or ministry. How about when you are restoring a relationship or rebuilding a sense of purpose in your life? The ways that you get others involved will be different, but the need to not bear the burden alone is just as great.

Delegation in these cases will include people who will pray for you and encourage you, some who will give the counsel you need, and others who will free up your time for relationships. When you get too busy with tasks, the first thing to go is usually time for relationships. There may be some tasks you'll need to delegate to others to open up the time you need to keep your relationships healthy.

I can't help but think about a lot of moms I know. The wonderful success of having a family easily becomes a growing to-do list of daily tasks. Bottle dispensed, diaper changed, asleep in crib—the parenting tasks are done for the day. Eighteen years later, it's dinner eaten, schoolwork finished, in by curfew. Yes, dads are also involved, but anyone who doesn't see that moms are bearing the brunt of this avalanche of tasks isn't paying attention.

For most of history, moms and dads didn't do it alone. Families stayed together in the same town for generations, so there were grandmas and grandpas, aunts and uncles, cousins and friends to help with the tasks. This is how it should be. We weren't meant to do even parenting alone.

There may be some people you need to reach out to who can support you in your parenting. Chaundel and I are forever grateful to people like Bob and Jan Snook, who became surrogate grandparents to our kids when our parents died at early ages. I'd argue that the greatest building project on earth is the building of children's lives and character in families. Of course we were not meant to do it alone.

What do you need to delegate to help you in your business, family, or ministry? God has given you this success, and he wants to accomplish great things through it. Who needs to join you in what God has given?

Let It Go

Let it go—these words are more than the title of the hit song from the Disney movie *Frozen!* There is a step beyond delegation—a third step for stewarding our successes—that many of us never get to, one that will allow a success given by God to truly become all it should be. When we delegate something to someone, it is often still under our control. We check up on them to be sure they're doing a good job in the task we've delegated.

Because we can only do so much, if we don't *let things go* as they grow, we will find ourselves overburdened. It's often our need to be in control of everything that causes us to feel out of control in life. The step beyond delegation is to release control into the hands of those we trust.

Parents must do this with children. As children grow up, we delegate to them more and more responsibility. There will come a day when they move out of our home and we release a measure of control over them. If we don't do this, they will not grow into the adult responsibilities and opportunities God has for them.

We've begun to call parents who cannot seem to release this control "helicopter parents." They are always hovering nearby, ready to rescue. The truth is, most of us want to be in the helicopter; most of us want to keep trying to control what we know we should release.

Releasing control is just as important in business or ministry. God has something for us to do next, but we cannot do what's next until we release what we are now doing. We need to learn the lesson from children who swing on monkey bars. You can hold on to two bars, but unless you release one, you can't swing to a third. Unless you release one, your arms will eventually get tired and you'll drop to the ground. Some of life's greatest lessons can be found right there on a playground!

We learn from Nehemiah that the key to releasing control is *deciding to trust*. You won't be able to release what is important to you without finding a person you know you can trust. Nehemiah 7:2 reads, "I put in charge of Jerusalem my brother Hanani, along with Hananiah the commander of the citadel, because he was a man of integrity and feared God more than most people do."

Notice the humble risk that Nehemiah took. He had been the one who put his life on the line when he asked the king if he could go back to Jerusalem to rebuild the wall. It was Nehemiah who led the people in the daily work, defeating the opposition. He alone was out in front making this project happen.

Then he put someone else in charge of the wall he had built.

He easily could have thought, *No one else is touching that wall. I built it.* And he would have crumbled under the pressure. He could lead by himself for the short term, but he needed others to come alongside him in leadership for the long term.

Nehemiah shows wisdom in two important ways as he releases a responsibility to someone. This is the wisdom that will prevent letting go from turning into a nightmare. The nightmare is that we release it to someone else, they don't do well, and it comes back to us worse than it was.

Our temptation then is to think, *I should have just kept doing it myself.* What we should think instead is, *I chose the wrong person or didn't prepare them well.* How can we choose better and prepare better? As a first step, choose integrity over skill.

Skill is important in a leader, without a doubt. But there are thousands of stories of those who had great skill but no integrity, and thus ruined a business, family, church, or ministry. Skill indicates they can do the job, but character is what tells us a person can be trusted with the responsibility to lead.

Find someone you know you can trust. Nehemiah chose his brother to be one of the leaders because he knew him so well. He also chose Hananiah, whom he had come to know well enough to see that he was "a man of integrity."

Not only do you need someone you know you can trust, but you also want somebody who you know can trust God. Hananiah was a man who "feared God more than most people do." One of the keys to great leadership is great humility. The place that great humility comes from is our trust in God.

As long as we think we're doing it ourselves, every success will only build our pride. Through trust in God, we recognize how dependent we are on his working through our work. One of the greatest Christian leaders in history, the apostle Paul, recognized this when he wrote, "Not that we are adequate in ourselves to consider anything as coming from ourselves, but our adequacy is from God" (2 Corinthians 3:5 NASB).

After you choose a person of integrity, it's just as important to give clear instructions. If you've ever been given a responsibility without guidance, you understand the value of instructions. Decide to overcommunicate rather than undercommunicate.

Nehemiah 7:3 reads, "I said to them [Hanani and Hananiah], 'The gates of Jerusalem are not to be opened until the sun is hot. While the gatekeepers are still on duty, have them shut the doors and bar them. Also appoint residents of Jerusalem as guards, some at their posts and some near their own houses.'" There is much to learn about giving clear instructions here.

The command to "shut the doors and bar them" reminds us that clear instructions don't assume anything. Nehemiah could have just told them to shut the doors, assuming they'd understand that it meant they should lock them with a bar. Instead of leaving this command to chance, Nehemiah tells them to shut and then bar the doors. What's the use of shutting the door if it can be easily pushed open? Clarity made sure the purpose was fulfilled in the task.

A story from Saddleback Church's early days serves as a reminder of the need for clarity in what we instruct. Years before our emphasis on health through the Daniel Plan, Saddleback had a standing order with a nearby baker for forty dozen donuts each weekend.

We were doing a wedding renewal for the whole church as a part of the services one weekend and decided to order wedding cake for everyone to enjoy. Realizing at the last minute that we wouldn't need all those donuts, someone called the baker and hurriedly told them, "You know that standing order we have? Well, cut it in half." The caller realized he should have taken the time to be clearer the next day when the full order of forty dozen donuts came—all sliced in half.

Through the right leaders and clear instructions, we can have greater confidence as we let something go. Even then, it's always a risk, but the greater risk is found in holding on for too long.

One of my greatest lessons in many years in a rapidly growing church is the need to let go. If we don't let go, we won't continue to grow. We'll stay stuck where we are. If we don't let go, the ministry or business won't continue to grow. It will stay dependent on us.

My strongest experience with this came with the letting go of teaching our midweek Bible studies. During my first ten years at Saddleback Church, I taught a weekly study through the Bible, first to a few dozen people and eventually seeing it grow to a few thousand. I'm a Bible teacher at heart, so what a privilege it was to teach God's Word to God's people!

As much as I enjoyed the people at this Bible study, the feeling began to grow in me that there were thousands more who needed to study God's Word who were not there. And I felt that what we were doing in these Bible studies was much the same as what we were doing on the weekends. People needed something different for their growth.

We were beginning to emphasize small groups more strongly, but I knew that as long as people were coming to midweek Bible study, they probably weren't going to join a small group. Their full schedules would make them feel they couldn't fit it all in. So I went to Rick Warren and suggested we stop doing midweek Bible study so more people could be in small groups. I knew that in a large church, people would not be able to grow spiritually without the relational interaction and accountability of a small group. I think Rick had been patiently waiting for me to come to this conclusion—one he had been seeing for some time.

So I let go of something I loved to do. And many of our members let go of a midweek service that was meaningful to them. In this case, the result was almost immediate. Up to that point, we had about eight hundred small groups meeting at Saddleback. That year, our number of small groups exploded to three thousand. We saw a tenfold increase when we let go of our midweek services and started Purpose Driven Life small groups.

Obviously, as wonderful as our midweek services were, they were a bottleneck to the greater thing God was looking to do. A. W. Tozer wrote, "In the kingdom of God, the surest way to lose something is to try to protect it, and the best way to keep it is to let it go."[2] The greatest stewardship of your successes often comes in this moment of letting it go.

Put It to Use

As a fourth step to building on your successes, you must *see the ways you can continue to be put to use*. Nehemiah 7 tells of the registering of the families who lived in Jerusalem. This was done because there was a problem: "Now the city was large and spacious, but there were few people in it, and the houses had not yet been rebuilt. So my God put it into my heart to assemble the nobles, the officials and the common people for registration by families" (Nehemiah 7:4–5).

The wall had been rebuilt, but the city inside that wall still needed to be rebuilt. Why rebuild the walls if the city wasn't going to be filled? So God put it into Nehemiah's heart to register the people so they could live, be protected, raise their families, and worship God in the city. God gave Nehemiah the idea that allowed the success of the rebuilding of the wall to be utilized for the blessing of God's people.

---

2. A. W. Tozer, *Born After Midnight* (1959; repr., Chicago: Moody, 2015), 117.

Before seeing what we can learn from the registration of the families, let's take a moment to look more closely at what it means for God to put something into our hearts. Just as with Nehemiah, God is going to put some things into your heart that allow you to build on the successes he has brought into your life. How does that happen? What does it feel like? If you don't know the answers to those questions, you might miss this all-important moment of direction.

When God puts something into your heart, it's the result of listening with a desire to obey. Nehemiah obeyed God by rebuilding the wall, and then he listened for what was next. That listening was prompted by noticing a need: the city was spacious, but there weren't enough people in it. From this, God put it into his heart to register the families. When God puts something into your heart, it is the key moment in building on the foundation of your successes.

Sometimes it comes in a practical idea that pops into your head; other times it's almost like an audible voice you hear from God; and other times it comes in the form of a conviction that gradually grows in you. The common denominator is an unusual certainty that this is what God wants you to do—a certainty always verified by the truth of God's Word and almost always by the encouragement of other believers.

When I became a pastor at Saddleback Church many years ago, it was because God put something into my heart. I was in my tenth year of pastoring the church in Marysville, the last five years of which had been spent rebuilding after the flood. Our family and the Warren family were together at a church conference. My wife, Chaundel, is Rick's younger sister, so we regularly looked for times to connect in the flow of ministry.

Before one of the conference sessions, Rick was sitting behind me, talking to our mutual friend Harry Williams. Rick didn't know

I was listening as he talked about his desire to make the next change in the structure of Saddleback's staff that would draw it more closely around God's five purposes for the church.

He'd have a pastor of membership, a pastor of maturity, a pastor of ministry, a pastor of mission, and a pastor of magnification. In this moment of holy eavesdropping, it was as though God was sending an arrow into my heart telling me I needed to talk to Rick about being the pastor of maturity at Saddleback Church.

It was not an audible voice, but it was a powerful impression like I've had only two or three times in my life. I knew that if I didn't talk to Rick, I'd be disobeying God. It was not a matter of me telling him, "The Holy Spirit said you have to hire me." Whether he said yes or no was his decision; I just knew I needed to ask. By God's grace, I came to Saddleback Church in 1991 to serve as pastor of maturity for ten years and then as teaching pastor in the years since.

These heart impressions may come in powerful ways such as this, or they may come in simpler ways. Many years ago, my friend Buddy Owens mentioned to me that I should take the studies I had taught at our midweek Bible study for many years and teach them online in a podcast. He said, "You could call it DriveTime Devotions."

I've now taught through most of the Bible in this ten-minute-a-day podcast, with tens of millions of downloads—all because of a heart impression that came from a brief conversation with a friend. While different from the powerful impression I had when I came to Saddleback, it was an idea that I knew came from God.

By God's grace, the teaching I let go of in midweek Bible study has now been multiplied to many others through this daily podcast. When you let it go, God often gives it back to you in a way that's greater than you expected.

Whether it's a powerful impression or an idea from a friend, what is God putting into your mind about how to build on the successes he has given you in your life?

For Nehemiah, the idea was to register the families. In so doing, he could see the resources that God had given him to use: the families who were available to live in the city. In its listing of name after name of those who were registered, chapter 7 is one of those "boring" parts of the Bible that many of us skip over as we read.

It was anything but boring for Nehemiah! In every name there was an opportunity. He saw where they could live, how the city could be built, and how the generations would be raised there. When we get to chapter 10 of Nehemiah, we're going to see how Nehemiah connected these people to God's purposes for the city through their dedication to God.

There is a powerful principle here concerning what happens when you look at the resources God has given you. When you do an inventory of the available resources, you start to move from "what if" to "what now." You begin to see how God can use the resources he has given to further build on the successes he has given.

When your successes aren't being utilized, you have some choices. You can live in frustration, quit in anger, or search for solutions. It's amazing how often the solutions are found in looking at the resources God has already given.

Nehemiah didn't waste his success. He searched for solutions so he could put to use what God had given. In the search for solutions, we see three key actions throughout the book of Nehemiah.

The first is *praise*. If we're going to build on the success God gives, the first thing we need to do is praise God for the success. As long as we think the success is ours, we won't be able to build as God wants us to build. We'll be filled either with pride that we've done so well or with discouragement that things are falling apart. As we praise God for the success, we recognize that *it's his*. This praise to God causes us to look forward in anticipation of what he wants to do next rather than looking backward in self-satisfaction or frustration.

Praise gets the focus off of what we can do and on what God can do.

The second action is *service*. Nehemiah recognized that God had not given him his position and success for his own sake. It was in serving others that he found the fulfillment of God's greatest goals for his life. Jesus said that even he, the Son of God, "did not come to be served, but to serve" (Mark 10:45).

God allowed us to rebuild that church in Marysville so the church could serve the community. He is restoring your marriage so you can serve him by serving others in that marriage. He restores your business so it can become a vehicle for loving God and others.

With this attitude of praise and the decision to serve, you next *evaluate your resources*. What gifts, opportunities, people, and talents has God given you to work with? The point is not to ask if you have enough. Almost always you will feel you don't have enough to do what God has put in your heart to do. The point is to look carefully at what you have and to put what you have to work.

David had only five smooth stones, and God was able to work with that to defeat a giant. Gideon had an army of just three hundred men, and God was able to work with that to defeat thousands. And don't forget a little boy who had only five loaves and two fish. Jesus was able to work with that to feed five thousand people.

You don't look at your resources to see if you have enough; you look at your resources to see what you can give. And it is always when you give those resources that don't seem nearly enough that God works in ways that are more than enough.

Whatever success God has given, he has given it for a reason, and that success is a part of the stewardship of your life. Use the success he gave of restoring your marriage to help strengthen others in their marriages. Build on the success he gave of restoring the relationship with one of your children by encouraging other parents. Serve God with the success he gave of rebuilding a business by using that business to serve others. As you do this, you are trusting God to finish the story he started.

BUILD ON YOUR SUCCESSES:
My First Steps

SECURE YOUR INVESTMENT

What is the one most important thing you need to do to secure your investment in what you are beginning to put together again?

DON'T DO IT ALONE

Who can you involve in supporting you?

Who can help you with accomplishing the details of what needs to be done?

Who can help you with strengthening the overall purpose of what you are doing?

LET IT GO

What do you need to release to someone you trust in order to do something new?

PUT IT TO USE

How can you give praise to God for what he has put together again?

How can you serve others out of what God has given you?

What resources has God given you to work with?

Chapter 6

CELEBRATE TO SUSTAIN YOUR JOY

Intense determination without celebration becomes your downfall

Joy comes from seeing the complete fulfillment of the specific purpose for which I was created and born again, not from successfully doing something of my own choosing.

Oswald Chambers

Every experience, even the most unwelcome, if offered to Jesus, can become your gateway to joy.

Elisabeth Elliot

Celebrate God all day, every day.

Philippians 4:4 MSG

Life did not turn out as expected for Liz and Gary Puffer. Things had been looking so good. They had two little boys, six and eight years old, who were filling their house with energy. Liz was fully engaged in raising these boys and in the life of the community. Gary was working in the aerospace industry, installing hydraulics for commercial and military projects, including the space shuttle. His life had just recently turned back to faith after years of struggling with addictions to drugs and alcohol.

Then came the news that Gary had a brain tumor. It was not cancerous, but it had slowly grown into much of his brain. He would require thirty-five hours of surgery and would be left with deafness in his left ear and partial paralysis on the left side of his face. Many months of recovery stretched out before him.

This would not be the only physical challenge that Liz and Gary would face together. In the years to come, he endured a heart attack and a stroke due to issues with blood clots. In his midfifties, Gary had to retire with disability, a very difficult choice for a man who wanted to work to support his family.

I asked them, "What do you do when life doesn't turn out as you expected?" Their answer wasn't a surprise. I've seen it evidenced in their lives many times. Liz said, "Instead of looking for how God could bless us, we looked for who we could bless." Out of their pain, they turned their hearts toward serving others.

That's not where we always turn when we are in pain, so I

asked them what caused them to turn toward serving rather than self-centeredness. It took them a moment to answer. Their first thought was that they simply couldn't have done anything else. As they reflected further, they realized it was the examples of serving they had witnessed that prompted them to serve others.

Gary remembered growing up in a pastor's home. The ways his dad served the community came back to him as he went through his health crises and the identity crisis of early retirement. He knows that Proverbs 22:6 has powerfully become true in his life: "Start children off on the way they should go, and even when they are old they will not turn from it."

Liz did not grow up in a Christian home. Yet she distinctly remembers the faith that was shown to her when her sister Robin died at the age of eighteen. One memory of a local pastor visiting their home and having the family hold hands in a circle as he prayed speaks to her even now of the powerful difference made by simple acts of serving others in love.

Liz and Gary are two of the most servant-hearted people I know. If you were to ask me whose servant gifts have most impacted Saddleback Church, it would be women like Liz Puffer and her predecessor on our pastoral care team, Renee Yapp. They have pastorally cared for more people in the hurt places of life than anyone I can think of. And Gary is often right there alongside Liz.

Years later, Liz's and Gary's examples of serving would have a powerful impact in the life of one of their boys. Their son Brandon became a major league relief pitcher with the Houston Astros, San Diego Padres, and San Francisco Giants. In 2008 he was pitching for the minor league Frisco Rough Riders, hoping to get back to the majors.

Dealing with his own addictions to drugs and alcohol, Brandon broke into someone's home. He was so intoxicated that he doesn't remember the events of that night. He was arrested and eventually sentenced to five years for his crime after pleading guilty. Nolan Ryan, the famous pitcher who had become a friend, spoke as a character witness for him at his trial. Brandon's lawyer told him that if he got sentenced in Texas, even with Nolan Ryan as a character witness, he needed to know that time in prison was a part of God's plan for his life.

Liz and Gary had to deal as parents with yet another twist in a life that wasn't turning out as they expected. They had been watching their son pitch in major league parks, and now they were visiting him in prison. Liz would go to the store and find herself unable to get out of the car. She just couldn't handle the thought of running into someone she knew. Eventually, they were able to trust God with this turn in their lives. They knew that God's will for Brandon would be done, even in the midst of these circumstances.

During his time in prison, Brandon had to choose the direction his life would take. As much as he wanted to get back to the major leagues, he began to see that goal as being only about his ego. He decided instead to follow his parents' examples and look for ways to serve.

He now works with the Nolan Ryan Foundation, helping young baseball prospects. He's able to serve them by showing them how to improve their skills. Even more importantly, his story serves as a warning of the traps they can all too easily fall into.

In many ways, the focus of Brandon's celebration has changed. He used to be celebrated by forty thousand fans in the stands for making the right pitch. Now he's choosing to celebrate the ways God is working through his life to make a difference as he serves others.

To continue to rebuild, we almost always face a change in what we celebrate and how we celebrate.

THE NEED FOR CELEBRATION

Many rebuild their wall only to find that it has crumbled! They accomplish the task only to find that they have been consumed by it. They have become so busy and successful that life is just no fun anymore. We are not meant to become unsmiling workaholics in order to put things together again. We can accomplish great tasks while still being able to enjoy life.

Celebration of what God is doing is one of the keys to putting it back together again in a way that lasts. If you can't celebrate, you're likely to repeat whatever caused you to have to rebuild in the first place. You may not face the same circumstances, but you'll find yourself stuck in the same places. It is celebration that gives continued strength for the changes God is working in your life.

Begin by embracing the truth that *you are made to celebrate.* Celebration is not your idea; it's God's idea. Some Christians seem to think they can have "joy" without enjoying anything. For them, serving God is serious business to be faced with a holy intensity that does not allow for a smile. This makes no sense. Being in the presence of the sacred does not mean we have to be sad all the time.

In Nehemiah 8:9, Nehemiah addresses this issue: "Nehemiah the governor, Ezra the priest and teacher of the Law, and the Levites who were instructing the people said to them all, 'This day is holy to the LORD your God. Do not mourn or weep.' For all the people had been weeping as they listened to the words of the Law."

We obviously can and sometimes should mourn in the presence of God. It's where we began in Nehemiah 1. There are times when we need to weep before the Lord. But the idea that the only way to have a sacred experience is with a mournful heart and a downcast

133

look is totally false. Enjoyment is God's idea. He gave us that capacity. He gave us those emotions.

CELEBRATION GROWS OUT OF WORSHIP

Worship is the vital key to the personal celebration and joy that enable us to endure in anything we have rebuilt.

In Nehemiah 8, the Israelites hold a great day of celebrating God in worship for all that he had done. Celebration cannot be divorced from worship, because it grows out of worship. The word *celebrate* comes from the Latin, meaning "to gather to honor." Our attitude of celebration is rooted in gathering with others and honoring God for what has happened. We can't truly celebrate without worshiping, because God is the one whom we most celebrate and the one who created us to celebrate.

It is an indictment on our times when the tie between celebration and worship is not immediately obvious. We live with a strange propensity toward celebrating everywhere but in worship. Personal devotional times are serious; our get-togethers with friends are where we celebrate with fun and laughter. Church worship services are somber and quiet; football games are filled with loud cheers.

We can celebrate apart from worship, but they will be celebrations that leave us wanting. As wonderful as it is to celebrate at a family gathering, sporting event, or business party, there is a longing for something more if these celebrations are removed from a life of worship. Celebration apart from the God who made us to celebrate is a temporary escape at best; celebration connected to the worship of God is an infinite source of joy.

This is not to say that we must sing hymns at baseball games. In a life of worship, we recognize at the deepest level that God made the green grass of the baseball field, gave the players their skills, and gave us the ability to enjoy it all.

While there are multiple places of celebration in our lives, an obvious place to begin to connect celebration and worship is in our worship together as a church. As a start, we must ask ourselves whether we celebrate when we worship. Many people who come to a worship service every week seem to be sadly lacking in the joy department.

If we're honest, the Sunday morning service in many churches is more like a funeral than a festival. Christians look like they've been baptized in vinegar and taken the Lord's Supper with lemon juice! Showing up on a Sunday morning is obviously not enough. Nehemiah shows us two vital attitudes for worship. Without these attitudes, celebration is reduced; with these attitudes, celebration is multiplied.

Worship with an Attitude of Unity

A vital aspect to joy-filled worship is *being in unity with others.* That unity is described in Nehemiah 8:1: "All the people came together as one in the square before the Water Gate." To increase your celebration in worship, enjoy the people you worship with.

That may sound easy—until you try it for a while. The problem is, the people you worship with are just as imperfect and sinful as you are. So the longer you worship with a group, the more you'll be irritated, disappointed, or even deeply hurt by those you are getting to know.

Some people try to solve this problem by constantly changing churches, looking for the perfect group of people to worship with.

After the first few weeks in a new church, it may look like they are going to be that flawless fellowship you've been looking for, but it doesn't take long to discover that they have just as many problems as the church you just left.

The next step down this road of disappointment with people is to decide to worship alone—maybe by being out in nature or by watching services online. At least that way you only have to deal with your own problems. While that may be true, you're also cheating yourself out of the joy that God intends to come out of worship with others.

Hebrews tells us to not forsake our gathering together, because it is out of the struggle of meeting *together* that the true richness of worship is found (Hebrews 10:25). Being with others in a spirit of unity has the power to lift you up when you are down—through their encouragement. It has the power to strengthen you when you are weak—through their love. It has the power to focus you on what's truly important—through your serving others.

Worshiping God with others causes us to gain needed perspective. In celebrating God, we have the unique opportunity to see ourselves for who we truly are—every one of us equally in need of the loving grace of God. Richard Foster wrote, "In celebration the high and the mighty regain their balance and the weak and lowly receive new stature."[1]

Too often we take the privilege and power of Christian fellowship for granted. I know I do. I was reminded of this when I visited our Saddleback campus in Berlin, Germany. After services end in most American churches, people leave in about two or three minutes. We are focused on getting to our cars so we can get the

---

1. Richard J. Foster, *Celebration of Discipline: The Path to Spiritual Growth* (San Francisco: HarperSanFrancisco, 1978), 168.

checkered flag in some imaginary race out of the parking lot. In Berlin, most of the church attenders were still talking for up to an hour after the service!

I asked a few people why they stayed so long, and they told me that less than 1 percent of the residents of Berlin are believers. For most of these people, no one else in their neighborhood, workplace, or school is a follower of Jesus. That hour after the service is the only Christian fellowship they get all week. They were hungry for what they lacked.

Sometimes we have a kind of "fast-food fellowship" in our relationships with other believers. Having fast-food restaurants on every corner causes us to drive by most of them and to stop as quickly as we can when we are hungry. In a similar way, having believers all around us often causes us to fail to value what we have or to give time to those relationships that are most important.

When you are not yet a believer, it is the responsibility of a church family to connect with and welcome you as you join them for worship. But once you become a follower of Jesus, it is your responsibility to connect with others. If you find yourself making your way into and out of church without talking to even one other person, you are cheating yourself out of the joy that God intends to grow out of our worship. Worship certainly must be focused upward toward God. And because we worship together, it also must be expressed outward toward each other.

To increase your celebration in worship, you must increase your enjoyment with the people you worship with. There will be many times when you won't want to go to church. When you choose to go anyway, you'll find those are the weeks you most needed to be in church. You were being tempted to not choose what you most needed, namely, to be around other people.

Worship with a Love for God's Word

The more you increase *your love for God's Word*, the greater your celebration in worship. The example of the people of Israel on the day of worship described in Nehemiah 8 shows that our love for God's Word is deepened as we recognize the significance of his Word.

If you go to a World Cup soccer final, you'll see an undeniable sense of celebration because of the significance of the event. In many stadiums around the world, the fans will stand for the entire match because it is so important. Nehemiah 8:5 reads, "Ezra opened the book. All the people could see him because he was standing above them; and as he opened it, the people all stood up."

Some churches stand for the Scripture reading, often pointing to this verse. Whether or not you stand is not the most important thing, although it can be a good thing. What is important is that a sense of significance is attached to God's Word. This is one of the attitudes that creates celebration in worship—the feeling that nothing is more important than what we're hearing in that moment from God's Word.

The Israelites' experience that day shows that for the significance of God's Word to be a part of worship, there is something that worship leaders must do and something that the worshiping congregation must do. Both have a responsibility.

The leaders must teach in a way that people can understand: "They [the Levites] read from the Book of the Law of God, making it clear and giving the meaning so that the people understood what was being read" (Nehemiah 8:8). If something is significant and yet we don't understand it, we just feel confused.

If I were to go to a World Cup soccer final, I would enjoy what was going on because I understand soccer. If I were to go to a World Cup cricket final, it would feel significant, but I'd be confused

138

because I don't understand cricket. There are bowlers, googlies, silly mid-offs, and dibbly dobblies—none of which I understand. I would need someone to sit with me and explain it all so I could enjoy the game.

When leaders make God's Word clear, the celebration of God is magnified. One of the most celebrative moments in worship is when a simple explanation of God's truth makes the light go on in our hearts! When we understand it, then we're able to live it.

As important as it was for the leaders to make the teaching understandable, it was what the people did that day that resulted in truly joyful worship: *they listened attentively to the Word.* Nehemiah 8:3 reads, "He [Ezra] read it aloud from daybreak till noon as he faced the square before the Water Gate in the presence of the men, women and others who could understand. And all the people listened attentively to the Book of the Law." They listened for five or six hours! One of the keys to understanding why some worship services are more filled with joy is attentive listening.

There's a difference between hearing and attentively listening. Suppose I'm reading the newspaper, and my wife, Chaundel, says something to me, and I respond, "Uh-huh, uh-huh," with my eyes still on the page. If she asks, "What did I say to you?" I *might* be able to repeat what she just said, but anyone would know I was not attentively listening. I may have heard the words, but I didn't have my mind and heart focused on what she was saying.

Attentively listening in worship is fixing your mind and heart on what God is saying to you. When you do that, the celebration increases in your worship experience. Then your joy adds to the sense of joy that everyone is experiencing in that service.

I'll never forget a worship experience in November 1993. After meeting in school auditoriums and gyms for twelve years,

Saddleback Church had moved to its first property two years before. Land in Orange County is expensive, so for the first two years on this property, we met in an open-air tent.

Even in the mild Southern California climate, we froze in the winter, burned up in the summer, and were almost blown away by the Santa Ana winds in the fall. It was time to build, and the church had been praying and worshiping as we prepared to give together toward the building that would be our new place of worship.

As we came together to celebrate the gifts that had been given, there was a deep sense of unity and strong attentiveness to our obedience to God's Word. The result was a spontaneous and powerful sense of celebration. I'll never forget an older pastor saying to me that day, "Don't forget what is happening here, Tom. These are the kinds of worship services that can inspire a generation." This is the power of celebration.

There is an inevitable response to this kind of celebration. Nehemiah 8:6 reads, "Ezra praised the LORD, the great God; and all the people lifted their hands and responded, 'Amen! Amen!' Then they bowed down and worshiped the LORD with their faces to the ground."

This verse reveals that true praise always results in an attitude of profound humility before God. You know God has given you what you do not deserve simply because of his love.

To express this humility, the Israelites bowed down and put their faces to the ground. There is something to be said for expressing physically what is happening to us spiritually in worship. I admit I sometimes struggle with physical expressions of praise or devotion in worship. Maybe it's my background, or maybe it's that these expressions can too often feel expected or copied.

I know I need to grow to see that the body and spirit are tied together in deeper ways than I imagine. Physical expressions of worship have the power to connect me spiritually and emotionally to what I'm singing or hearing. Whether it's bowing your head, raising your hands, or just lifting your eyes ever so slightly toward heaven, take the risk to express outwardly what God is speaking to your heart.

WORSHIPING IN WAYS WE MAY NOT HAVE EXPECTED

Before we leave our look at celebration and worship, there's an issue we must address. Sometimes we lose our sense of celebration in worship because our worship becomes *routine*. Yes, there is something comforting about the same routine of worship every week. Yet it is also true that the routine can cause us to lose our sense of excitement and anticipation in celebrating God.

God has designed our human minds to need both routine and variety. In accordance with our personality, we'll enjoy one of those more than the other. Still, we need both.

There are three specific directions for celebration in Nehemiah 8 that we may not expect to find in God's Word—and these directions give us some ideas about how to worship in ways we may not have expected.

First, Nehemiah tells the people to *feast*. God considers feasting a part of celebrating:

> Nehemiah said, "Go and enjoy choice food and sweet drinks, and send some to those who have nothing prepared. This day is holy to our Lord. Do not grieve, for the joy of the LORD is your strength."

The Levites calmed all the people, saying, "Be still, for this is a holy day. Do not grieve."

Then all the people went away to eat and drink, to send portions of food and to celebrate with great joy, because they now understood the words that had been made known to them.

Nehemiah 8:10–12

God gave us our taste buds, and they're a great gift for celebrating. It is a sin to worship food. And it is equally a sin not to be willing to celebrate with food. God commands us throughout Scripture to celebrate with everything he has made, which includes the food he has made. First Timothy 6:17 declares that God "richly provides us with everything for our enjoyment."

You can worship God with a fast, and you can also worship with a feast. A feast is an excellent tool for celebration. This is clear throughout the Bible: in all the feasts of the Old Testament, in Jesus' first miracle that took place at a wedding feast, in the Passover feast Jesus had with his disciples, and in the fact that when we get to heaven, we're going to celebrate forever in the great wedding feast of the Lamb.

Eating unhealthy food all the time is obviously wrong, and so is thinking that denying yourself food that tastes good somehow makes you more spiritual. You can have a Daniel Plan feast.[2] Celebrate a spiritual milestone in someone's life or a great thing that God has done by having a feast together. Invite some friends who are not yet believers to join you for this feast. It's one of the greatest ways to help these friends experience what it means to celebrate God.

---

2. The Daniel Plan combines exercises in the five areas of food, friends, fitness, focus, and faith to lead to better health (Rick Warren, Daniel Amen, and Mark Hyman, *The Daniel Plan: 40 Days to a Healthier Life* (Grand Rapids: Zondervan, 2013).

God first tells the Israelites to feast. Second, he tells them to *share*. Sharing is an important part of celebrating. Look again at Nehemiah 8:10: "Go and enjoy choice food and sweet drinks, and send some to those who have nothing prepared. This day is holy to our Lord."

Nothing can cut into your joy as quickly as selfishness.

Many of us are surrounded by material blessings that no longer seem to bring joy. When that happens, the first question to ask is, "Who can I share with?" The greatest joy in life comes not from what you have but from what you give. If you're just holding on to things, they'll eventually sour in your hands, just like the manna spoiled for the people of Israel in the wilderness (Exodus 16).

The third thing Nehemiah directs the people to do is to *be still*. Nehemiah 8:11–12 reads, "The Levites calmed all the people, saying, 'Be still, for this is a holy day. Do not grieve.' Then all the people went away . . . to celebrate with great joy."

An expression of celebration is not always found in the shouting; it's often found in the stillness. It's a celebration to be quietly caught up in a moment of beauty, in the love of those around you, or in a spirit of gratitude. Sometimes you need to be still in the presence of the Lord with a deep sense of appreciation for who he is.

When we think of being still before the Lord, we most often think of a solemn and serious stillness. That is one way to be still before God, yet here we see another way. This is a *celebrative and joyful* stillness.

There are times when joy stills our hearts. Charles Spurgeon wrote, "It would be very difficult to draw a line between holy wonder and *real worship*; for when the soul is overwhelmed with the majesty of God's glory, though it may not express itself in song or even utter its voice with bowed head in humble prayer, yet it silently adores."[3] Perhaps the most prolific speaker and writer of his generation, Spurgeon understood the value of adoring silence before God.

When I'm singing with others in worship, I sometimes enter these moments where I just need to be still. The joy of hearing others' voices fills my heart to a place where my greatest expression of celebration is not in singing louder but in being still and listening to the voices around me. When your heart becomes full, it can cause you to be still—the kind of stillness a parent feels when they first hold their child. There are no words; there is just joy.

Through being still in celebration, you'll often find yourself experiencing an exchange of emotions. In the stillness, you exchange your anxiety for a sense of trust in God, your guilt for a depth of gratitude for God's forgiveness, your fear for a moment of faith, your grief for genuine joy.

To this point in our look at celebration, we've focused primarily on worship. That's intentional! Without worship, you will never get to the place of genuine celebration, the kind of celebration that energizes your lives. Celebration begins with worship.

CELEBRATION RESULTS IN NEW STRENGTH

In the midst of this great day of celebration for Nehemiah and God's people, we come across this sentence in Nehemiah 8:10: "The joy of the LORD is your strength." These familiar words hold the key to the kind of strength we're all looking for.

Notice that it's the joy *of the Lord*. Nehemiah isn't talking about joy that you somehow try to manufacture from within; he's talking

---

3. Charles H. Spurgeon, *Evening by Evening: A New Edition of the Classic Devotional Based on the Holy Bible, English Standard Version* (Wheaton, IL: Crossway, 2007), 34.

about the joy that the Lord gives. If you try to force your hearts to have this strength-giving joy, you'll end up more tired than when you began.

How do we get the joy of the Lord into our lives? It's the joy of the Lord, so obviously we must look to what the Lord says about this. In John 15–17, we hear the Lord Jesus talking to his followers about the ways he gives this joy. If we want new strength, we must do the things he told us to do in these verses—and we must do them with a focus on the fact that he wants to use these things to bring us joy.

If you've been a follower of Christ for any time, you know how easy it is to lose your focus on the joy. You find yourself grinding away at spiritual habits, trying to become more powerful, when the real intent is that you become more joyful. Feeling powerful is not your strength; the joy of the Lord is your strength. This is the truth that may very well hold the secret to the life of faith that you've been longing for.

In John 15:11, Jesus says, "I have told you this so that my joy may be in you and that your joy may be complete." What had he just told them that would give this joy? In verse 9, Jesus said, "Remain in my love." To experience the joy of the Lord means you stay connected to Christ. Depend on him for your daily needs, and recognize that the significance of your life comes only from him.

Then, in John 15:10, 12, Jesus says that to stay connected to him, we must keep his command to love one another. To experience the joy of the Lord means we stay connected to other Christians.

This may seem like too simple a formula for joy: stay connected to God; stay connected to others. But it's not a formula; it's a relationship with God and others. And there is nothing simple about relationships! A loss of joy in your life is *always* a call to get closer to God and to get closer to other believers.

In John 16:20 (NLT), Jesus continues to talk about joy: "I tell you the truth, you will weep and mourn over what is going to happen to me, but the world will rejoice. You will grieve, but your grief will suddenly turn to wonderful joy." That's real-world joy. The joy of the Lord is not permanently painting a happy smile on your face and pretending everything is OK. Sometimes everything is *not* OK.

Jesus says you're going to grieve; you're going to face difficulties in this life. But your grief can be turned to joy, because his joy surpasses any grief you can face. Please know that I don't intend to minimize your grief in saying that. *I'm maximizing the joy of the Lord.* It's eternal. It covers every grief we have to face.

"The joy of the LORD is your strength." Joy gives the strength you've been looking for. If your strength for rebuilding is failing, don't try to become more determined. Instead, look to have greater joy.

This is the secret that many never learn, so they keep failing again and again. They try to become more determined but don't feel like being more determined, and even if they become determined, all they feel is more determined. And in determination alone a certain kind of weariness starts to set in. That's because determination is not where your real strength is; the joy of the Lord is your strength.

Your determination will eventually wear out—for some of us, it will happen sooner than it will for others. The joy of the Lord will *never* run out; it is an inexhaustible supply of strength for living. You cannot do the work of the Lord without the joy of the Lord.

Celebration is not just something you do when all of the rebuilding is finished. Celebration gives the strength you need all along the way. So don't wait until all is finished to celebrate; start today. Since the joy of the Lord is your strength, for every day you need strength, you also need joy.

What do you think of when you hear the word *joy*? Sometimes the misreading of one word can make all the difference.

Years ago, Chaundel and I were on our way to a meeting of churches at the convention center in Riverside. We left a little late and then got lost in the midst of a bunch of citrus-named streets in that part of town. Orange and Lemon and Grapefruit Streets all seemed to blend together.

Finally, I saw a huge sign on the corner that read "Riverside County Convention Center." We found a parking place on the street near a side door, jumped out of the car, and rushed up to the door, only to find it locked. We pulled at the door several times, hoping someone would hear the banging and let us in, but no one came.

As we started around to the front of the building, we passed by the large sign. I saw I had read it wrong. It wasn't Riverside County Convention Center; it was Riverside County *Corrections* Center. We had been trying to break into the county jail!

Fortunately, we weren't arrested. We finally made our way to the convention center, a little late and having learned a huge lesson on the importance of a single word.

When you read the word *joy*, I hope you don't see the word *job*. This is not a matter of it being your job to be happy in Jesus. It's a gift he wants to give you. It's not the joy of you that is your strength; it's the joy of *the Lord* that is your strength.

That joy starts in celebrative worship. Since it's the joy of the Lord, you won't find it apart from celebrating with the Lord. In that celebration, you are strengthened to see what God has rebuilt last and even become a blessing to others in ways you would have never imagined.

CELEBRATE TO SUSTAIN YOUR JOY:
My First Steps

CELEBRATION GROWS OUT OF WORSHIP

Here are some simple steps that can make a huge impact:

- If you haven't been attending worship with others, start there.
- If you need to set something right with someone you worship with, do it today.
- The next time you worship, honor Scripture by writing down one thing you sense God is guiding you to do through the Bible verses that are read and taught.
- Share with someone else what God has done in you through a worship experience.
- Be still—try two minutes of just sitting quietly before God. Instead of talking, just listen.

CELEBRATION RESULTS IN JOY

Ask yourself whether you are trying to gain strength by feeling powerful or whether you are trusting God for his strength by being joyful.

Memorize these words from Nehemiah 8:10: "The joy of the LORD is your strength."

Let these eight words run through your mind several times during the day—both when you feel strong and when you feel weak.

Chapter 7

DEDICATE IT TO GOD

What is dedicated to God is what will last

Resolved, never to do any manner of thing, whether in soul or body, less or more, but what tends to the glory of God.

**Number four of the seventy resolutions
of Jonathan Edwards**

The trouble is that relying on God has to begin all over again every day as if nothing had yet been done.

C. S. Lewis

I appeal to you therefore, brethren, and beg of you in view of [all] the mercies of God, to make a decisive dedication of your bodies [presenting all your members and faculties] as a living sacrifice, holy (devoted, consecrated) and well pleasing to God, which is your reasonable (rational, intelligent) service and spiritual worship.

Romans 12:1 AMP, classic edition

You know the name Michelangelo, but have you heard of Colalucci? Michelangelo created some of the world's greatest and most familiar works of art, including the ceiling and altar wall of the Sistine Chapel. Gianluigi Colalucci was the chief restorer of the great artist's work in what may be one of the most significant art restoration projects in history.

A look at the work of both the painter and the restorer tells us something about the patience it takes to restore. The southern and northern walls of the Sistine Chapel were painted from 1481 to 1483, the ceiling from 1508 to 1512, the altar wall from 1536 to 1541, and the eastern wall in 1572 and 1574. The total time to paint was twelve years. The restoration project, begun by Colalucci in June 1980, was unveiled by Pope John Paul II on April 8, 1994. That adds up to fourteen years. The restoration took longer than the original painting!

This begs the question, Why restore it at all? If it takes so long to restore something, why not just throw it away and start over? The answer in the case of the Sistine Chapel is obvious: it was restored because it is a priceless work of art. You are the same—a work of creation of immeasurable value to God! The restoration of a relationship, career, business, or dream is priceless to God. To throw it away would be as foolish as rolling white paint over the images of God and Adam in the Sistine Chapel because it would be quicker and easier to start fresh.

Never forget that in whatever you are putting back together, the most significant restoration is *what God is doing in you*. Through every circumstance, he is working to bring into your life more of the character of Christ—the love, grace, hope, and joy of Jesus.

As Gianluigi Colalucci reflects on his experiences as chief restorer, he describes carefully how he undertook the work of restoring the face of Adam:

> I was able to proceed with the solvent mixture, which was gelatinous and adhered to the fresco even in the middle of the ceiling. I applied it with a brush, left it to do its work for three minutes, stopwatch in hand, and then began to remove it with the small sponge soaked in water . . . The ugly mass of substances slowly disappeared beneath my hands to reveal a pattern of brushstrokes of pure colour closely interwoven so as to create or indeed sculpt the shape of the face, now able to breathe again . . . I paused in enchantment before this piece of painting, which had regained its highly delicate colouring . . . I stepped down from the low wooden dais and sat down to look up in delight at that spectacle, thinking that in spite of everything, this was the finest profession in the world.[1]

Restoring the face of Adam is a compelling picture of what God wants to do in each of us. The Bible often presents Adam as the representative of the entire human race, because his sin brought the need for restoration to all of us. That, of course, is not the end of the story. In the love and sacrifice of Jesus, we are all offered restoration of a relationship with God. Romans 5:18 (NLT) puts it this way: "Yes, Adam's one sin brings condemnation for everyone,

---

1. Gianluigi Colalucci, *Michelangelo and I: Facts, People, Surprises, and Discoveries in the Restoration of the Sistine Chapel* (Milan, Italy: 24 Ore Cultura, 2016), 132–33.

but Christ's one act of righteousness brings a right relationship with God and new life for everyone."

Through the love of Christ, God is restoring the work of art that is you. He is causing you to look more and more like Jesus every day. It is often slow work, but he is patient. Look carefully, and you can picture him gently wiping away the dirt and grime of the past, being careful not to destroy the underlying beauty he created in you. The promised completion of this project is almost beyond our imagination: "Just as each of us now has a body like Adam's, so we shall some day have a body like Christ's" (1 Corinthians 15:49 LB). God will bring out the full color of the masterpiece he has created you to be—and all will see that this beauty is because of Christ. This is the glory of God.

The truth of what God is doing in each of us leads directly to our need to dedicate what we are doing to God. To dedicate is to decide that something will be used for the sake of God's glory. When we recognize that God is working toward this glorious restoration in each of us, it becomes much easier to dedicate every circumstance of life to him.

For whatever is built or rebuilt to stay strong, it must be dedicated to God. To have a strong family, you must dedicate it to God. To have a strong business or church or life, you must dedicate it to God. Without dedication, you will see what you have built begin to decay; with dedication, you will see it continue to stay strong.

Dedication is a vital step for those who want to see what they've rebuilt remain. Far too many people trust God for the strength to restore a relationship or career, only to take it back to themselves once the hard work of rebuilding is done. In our desperation to avoid failure, we trust God, but once the crisis passes, we begin to trust ourselves again.

The people of Israel went through this pattern repeatedly. They would trust God; things would improve; they would take it back to themselves; things would fall apart; they had to trust God again—the same pattern over and over again.

The key to not seeing that pattern happen is found in *dedicating it all to God*. Nehemiah again is our example. He knew the wall wouldn't be truly completed until it had been dedicated. The dedication was not some nice little celebration ceremony at the end of the project; it was an all-important part of the rebuilding. Dedication recognized who the wall belonged to and who would get the credit for its usefulness.

Unless dedication is a part of your everyday life, you're going to feel like you're living only a half-life, because the purpose of life grows out of dedication. It's out of your dedication of whatever God has put into your hands that you recognize why it's there and what it can be used for.

Nehemiah gives four specific descriptions of what goes into the kind of dedication that results in this fullness of life. Some of what he presents may surprise you. All of it will challenge you.

DEDICATION BEGINS WITH THANKSGIVING

Nehemiah places *thanksgiving* at the very beginning: "At the dedication of the wall of Jerusalem, the Levites were sought out from where they lived and were brought to Jerusalem to celebrate joyfully the dedication with songs of thanksgiving and with the music of cymbals, harps and lyres" (Nehemiah 12:27).

If you can't thank God for it, you can't dedicate it to God. If your attitude is, "God, I hate my job, but I dedicate it to you because I know that's what I'm supposed to do," you're not really dedicating it to God; you're just using spiritual words to tell God how much he's let you down.

If instead you say with a humble heart, "God, I'm struggling in my job, but even in that struggle, I thank you for that job and I dedicate it to you," that's an entirely different attitude. That's an honest attitude of thanksgiving.

There are two specifics we learn from Nehemiah about dedication and thanksgiving.

First, *thanksgiving leads the way*. As we see with a number of leaders in the Old Testament, Nehemiah had the choirs that were giving thanks lead the way on this day of dedication—not the officials or the soldiers, but the choirs. In Nehemiah 12:31, we read, "I had the leaders of Judah go up on top of the wall. I also assigned two large choirs to give thanks. One was to proceed on top of the wall to the right . . ." And then in verse 38, we read, "The second choir proceeded in the opposite direction. I followed them on top of the wall, together with half the people."

Thankful joy took the lead. Dedicated people have learned to let thanks lead the way in their lives. We mistakenly think that thanksgiving follows our successes; instead, it usually precedes them. We give thanks to God for something seemingly small, and out of that thanksgiving, he does something even greater.

The second specific is that *thanksgiving must be heard*. In Nehemiah 12:43, we read, "On that day they offered great sacrifices, rejoicing because God had given them great joy. The women and children also rejoiced. The sound of rejoicing in Jerusalem could be heard far away." It's not really thanksgiving unless it's heard, unless we can tell somebody else about it.

Dedicated people not only feel their thanksgiving; they express it. The choirs remind us that one of the ways to express it is through singing. The Bible commands us in the New Testament to express our thanksgiving through "psalms, hymns, and songs from the

Spirit" (Ephesians 5:19). This is commanded for all of us, not an optional activity for only the really good singers. This is not a matter of how well you sing, but of what singing is doing for your heart. If you think you don't sing very well, so "I'll just listen to everybody else sing," you're missing out on one of the great things God wants to do in your heart as you worship.

You can also express thanks by telling people why you're praising God for what he's done in your life. For instance, "I'm grateful to God for the way he's been using others to encourage me this week." You can share your thanksgiving by writing about it in a social media post or blog. As you express it beyond yourself, it becomes more a part of yourself and impacts the hearts of others.

In the flood we experienced, all of our possessions were under water and mud for a couple of weeks. This included our computers and the program and data disks. In that day, the drives were 5$^1/_4$-inch floppies. (Just writing this is making me feel old!) Along with various games and programs, many of the disks contained a couple of years of my sermons and the data of several companies served by Chaundel's home bookkeeping business. Our backups at that time were hard copies in file cabinets that were also underwater.

We took these mud-encrusted disks to several computer repair shops, and they just laughed at us. Not having anything to lose, we took the thin circles of plastic out of their sleeves, carefully washed off the mud, dried them, and put them into new sleeves.

Chaundel told the story to the church: "When we put those drives in a new computer, not one of the programs worked and not one of the games. But *every word* of Tom's sermons was saved. *Every number* for my bookkeeping business was recovered!" As people cheered with celebration, their dedication was deepened because Chaundel shared her praise.

Right now, picture a person truly dedicated to his or her task. Is he or she smiling? When we picture dedication, we tend to picture a grimace of determination on someone's face. Dedication is obviously serious business. But it is serious business that takes place with thankfulness and joy. *Dedication begins with thankful joy.* If you don't picture that as a part of dedication, you're not going to be able to live a dedicated life.

We've been talking about giving thanks. Let's spend a few minutes putting it into practice before we move on.

In these moments, tell God thank you. Thank him for those things that come to your mind right now. Maybe it's your family and the blessings God has given. Maybe it's ministry opportunities that allow you to make a difference in this world. Maybe it's the way God is meeting a practical need in your finances or for a job. As you thank God, recognize that your expression of gratitude is part of the dedication of your heart to him in thankful joy.

DEDICATION IS SHOWN BY PURIFICATION

As people whom God is using for his purposes, *our dedication is shown in our purification*: "When the priests and Levites had purified themselves ceremonially, they purified the people, the gates and the wall" (Nehemiah 12:30). How do you purify yourself for God's purposes? The truth is, you don't purify yourself. God is the one who purifies you. Without getting into lengthy details, even the purification done by these Levites looked forward to Jesus and the purification he would bring.

You can become purified for God's purpose by *recognizing what Jesus did* for you on the cross. Do not try to purify yourself. You can't do it, because you're impure. Something that is impure cannot make something that is pure. Jesus is pure, so when you look to him and trust in what he did for you, he is your purification. In his prayer for his disciples, Jesus said, "And I give myself as a holy sacrifice for them so they can be made holy by your truth" (John 17:19 NLT).

Because of what Jesus did on the cross, you begin to live a holy, dedicated life. This means *allowing God to take out of your life those things that don't belong.* Paul points to some of these in his letter to the Ephesians: "Let there be no sexual immorality, impurity, or greed among you. Such sins have no place among God's people. Obscene stories, foolish talk, and coarse jokes—these are not for you. Instead, let there be thankfulness to God" (Ephesians 5:3–4 NLT). Just as importantly, becoming purified for God's purpose means *allowing God to put into your life those things that truly do belong.*

Purification is not only not doing certain things. Some people think that being pure just means you don't do this or that, and so you're pure. If that were true, the purest people in the world would be *dead* because they don't do anything. Of course purity has something to do with what you don't do—the sins you don't commit. But it also has something to do with what you choose to do—the obedience you exhibit toward God.

Purity is seen in *what you pursue.* What are you chasing after? If you're trying to be pure only by not doing certain things, you've missed most of what purity is all about, and you're engaged in a self-defeating process. The only way to run away from what's wrong is to run toward what is right. Dedication and purity are seen more in what you pursue than in what you don't do.

In Nehemiah's day, everything was a part of this dedication to purity. The people, the gates, and the wall—the priests and the Levites purified it all. The greatest danger to our dedication lies in the false idea that we can segment our lives into the dedicated and nondedicated—that when I'm at church, I'm dedicated; when I'm at work, I'm maybe not so dedicated. And when I'm with certain friends, I'm not dedicated at all.

Dedication Is an All-or-Nothing Proposition

Thinking of dedication as an all-or-nothing proposition is deeply discouraging to many, because we see ourselves on the "nothing" side of that equation. We are well aware of our struggles with sin. Let me give three brief words of encouragement if you see yourself as someone who loves Jesus but could never be dedicated to him with this kind of purity.

First, *you are not alone*. We all struggle with sin; we are all in need of a Savior. The apostle John wrote these words in the opening chapter of his first letter: "If we claim to be without sin, we deceive ourselves and the truth is not in us" (1 John 1:8).

Second, *you have hope*. Because of the gift of purity that Jesus died to offer you, you can in this moment be as dedicated to God as any other Christian. The path to that dedication is found in the next verse in 1 John: "If we confess our sins, he is faithful and just and will forgive us our sins and purify us from all unrighteousness" (1 John 1:9). Confession, not perfection, is the road to purity for followers of Jesus.

Third, *you can begin to live out this dedication in the small things*. The British preacher G. Campbell Morgan said, "The year is made up of minutes. Let these be watched as having been dedicated to God. It is in the sanctification of the small that hallowing of the large is secure."[2]

---

2. Quoted in Patrick Kavanaugh, "Are You Vegetating or Worshiping?" in *Times of Refreshing: A Worship Ministry Devotional*, ed. Tom Kraeuter (Lynnwood, WA: Emerald Books, 2002), 80.

You dedicate the next year to God by dedicating the next minute. You dedicate your career to God by dedicating the next task, however small. You dedicate your love for your family to God by dedicating the next conversation.

Remember Chad and Julie—the couple whose marriage restoration we looked at in chapter 2. Knowing how difficult it can be to keep a marriage growing over the long haul, I asked them how they kept it dedicated to God. Julie's response is an example of how dedication in the little things quickly becomes a big thing.

Julie said, "For me it was a matter of changing who I talked to. I used to call a friend who would agree with me every time I was angry at Chad. I decided that part of my dedication would be to talk to God about it and not the person who would build my feelings of anger.

"We had an argument sitting in the car, and Chad got out. My phone was sitting in my lap, and I so wanted to pick it up and call someone. I prayed, 'God, you told me to go to you, but I really want to call someone right now.' As I was praying, Chad got back in the car. He had never done this—he stayed away when we argued. I didn't know what to say. And then he apologized! It freaked me out."

It may be helpful here to mention a major controversy that occurred during the restoration of the Sistine Chapel. As the art began to be cleaned, many people were uncomfortable with the vibrant colors that began to emerge. Without fully exploring the details of this controversy, one thing that is certain is that the darker hues of a ceiling that had been covered by years of grime had become more familiar than the original. So people fought against the change.

This same discomfort happens as God restores our hearts and minds. We've become comfortable with old ways of thinking and doing, and so the restoration at first feels unfamiliar, scary, and somehow wrong. We're afraid of the beauty because we've gotten used to the dirt. We're afraid of the light because we've gotten used to the dark. It's natural to fear the new thing that God wants to do, because we all fear the unfamiliar. It's exhilarating when we begin to embrace the new thing that God is doing, because it's what we were created to be.

DEDICATION IS EXPRESSED IN GIVING

Dedication is expressed by *giving back to God out of what he's given to you*. God restores your marriage, not just so you can enjoy that marriage for yourself, but so you can now give back to God out of that marriage. God renews your family so you can give back to God out of that family. God rebuilds your career so now you can give back to God out of that career. He restores your finances, not just so you have more money, but so you can give back to him.

Giving is at the heart of dedication. It is the giving of our time, our possessions, our talents, and our concern that adds up to the giving of ourselves.

As we look at what the Israelites gave on this day of dedication, we see specifically how they gave their possessions:

At that time men were appointed to be in charge of the storerooms for the contributions, firstfruits and tithes. From the fields around the towns they were to bring into the storerooms the portions required by the Law for the priests and the Levites, for Judah was pleased with the ministering priests and Levites . . . So in the days of Zerubbabel and of Nehemiah, all Israel contributed the daily portions for the musicians and the gatekeepers. They also set aside the portion for the other Levites, and the Levites set aside the portion for the descendants of Aaron.

Nehemiah 12:44, 47

Of course, possessions aren't the only thing we give. Yet apart from the giving of those things God has placed in our hands, all other types of giving tend to wither as well. It is also true that the simple act of material giving opens the door to many other blessings in our lives, both now and in eternity. The Israelites' example teaches us four things about how giving becomes an expression of our dedication.

In all honesty, I wondered about including this section of teaching from Nehemiah. I was concerned it might sound too much like a class on tithing in the middle of a book on rebuilding. I decided to include it because of how often I've seen the simple act of the giving of possessions open the door to greater faith. In our materialistic age, there's something about giving that multiplies our faith like nothing else can. Over the years, I've received not just hundreds but thousands of testimonies to this truth.

First, *give obediently.* The Israelites gave the portions required by law. The reason we give is because God commands us to give. God wants us to give because he's a giver: "God so loved the world that he gave his one and only Son" (John 3:16). Giving is not a legalistic requirement; it is a loving obedience.

Second, *give responsibly.* The Israelites appointed some to be in charge of the gifts to make sure those gifts were used for God's purposes. They made sure the gifts were not lost and that no one took them to use for themselves. We give responsibly when we plan our giving and when we give to a church that we know will use what we give for God's purposes.

Third, *give cooperatively.* The Israelites *all* gave—it wasn't just

Putting It Together Again When It's All Fallen Apart

a few rich people. If we're not careful, we can begin to feel that those who have a lot can give the most. Jesus teaches very clearly that those who seem to have the least are the ones who can really give the most. The most honored sacrificial gift ever was a widow's two small coins. Jesus said no one had given like her because she gave everything she had (Luke 21:1–4).

If you feel you don't have enough to give to make a difference, you need to recognize that God is not looking at the amount; he's looking at your heart. That's why you give in the first place. God wants the obedience of your heart that the gift represents. Because God's accounting is different from ours, every gift is equally important. We give cooperatively because we all have a part in what God is doing.

Finally, *give sacrificially.* The Israelites offered great sacrifices on that day of dedication. They didn't look to give the least they could possibly give to be respectable; they gave the most they could possibly give because of their respect for God's greatness. Whatever sacrifices we make, God blesses us in return. But in the moment of giving, it doesn't always feel that way. In that moment, there is a decision to sacrifice.

Give obediently, responsibly, cooperatively, and sacrificially. Giving is a part of having a spirit of dedication. A spirit of dedication is vital to seeing what you've rebuilt remain.

DEDICATION MUST BE REFRESHED

We learn from Nehemiah that *dedication has to be refreshed regularly.* As we've been reading through these sections of Nehemiah, it may seem like these Israelites are a perfectly dedicated bunch of

164

God followers. As we read Nehemiah 13, we see that they struggled with achieving a lasting dedication.

What do you do when your dedication seems to wane? You can resign yourself to defeat; you can design yourself an excuse; or you can assign yourself a new commitment. The truth is, dedication must be refreshed regularly for all of us.

Nehemiah points us to the process you will go through to refresh your dedication—a process you will face many times in your life of faith.

Stop Skirting the Issue

The process begins with a decision to stop skirting the issue. In 13:11, Nehemiah writes, "So I rebuked the officials and asked them, 'Why is the house of God neglected?' Then I called them together and stationed them at their posts." The officials were neglecting some of the things that had caused their success, and Nehemiah called them on it. In chapter 1 of this book, we learned that the first step in putting anything together again is admitting there's a problem. Now we've come full circle: once again the Israelites must face a problem.

When you start to pretend that a problem isn't a problem, you really have a problem! You know you're denying reality when you're not able to talk about something or you hope that no one notices anything. That's the point where you need to be honest with yourself. Quit skirting the issue, and ask God to help you begin to dedicate your life to him anew.

Quit Compromising with Your Enemy

The next step is to quit compromising with your enemies. Compromise is the great enemy of commitment. We slowly compromise our way out of dedication. There's almost never one big decision that we make to not be committed; our downfall comes in a series of little compromises.

Let's learn from how Nehemiah handled this tendency to compromise:

> But while all this was going on, I was not in Jerusalem, for in the thirty-second year of Artaxerxes king of Babylon I had returned to the king. Some time later I asked his permission and came back to Jerusalem. Here I learned about the evil thing Eliashib had done in providing Tobiah a room in the courts of the house of God. I was greatly displeased and threw all Tobiah's household goods out of the room. I gave orders to purify the rooms, and then I put back into them the equipment of the house of God, with the grain offerings and the incense.
>
> **Nehemiah 13:6–9**

Perhaps you remember from Nehemiah 2 that Tobiah and Sanballat were the two great opponents of the rebuilding of the wall. Eliashib had given Tobiah a room in the courts of God's house. Here we see the very guy who had been an enemy of rebuilding now somehow having secured a room in one of the courts that had been rebuilt.

Maybe Tobiah paid a handsome sum of money for it, and people thought, *This is a great deal.* Maybe he convinced them it would be good politics. For whatever reason, the equipment for the house of God is in some closet somewhere while Tobiah enjoys this room.

The lesson here is this: the enemy will keep trying to move back in. This is why you must quit compromising and get back to a place of commitment. If you reengage with the friends who tore down your marriage, once you restore your marriage, they're going to try to tear it down again. If you begin to flirt with the habit that caused your addiction, you'll find yourself falling again.

Stop compromising with your enemies! Nehemiah didn't say, "Let's just move a few things out; maybe we can share the room." He simply threw all of Tobiah's household goods out. Then he put the equipment for the house of God back into that room. The action to take is obvious: You've allowed some bad things to move back into your life. Throw them out! Move the things of God back in!

Choose to Remove Opportunities for Sin

The third step in the process of refreshing your dedication is to make the choice to remove opportunities for sin. Remove them before you get to the place where you've let the bad things move in. Take a look at what happened:

> When evening shadows fell on the gates of Jerusalem before the Sabbath, I ordered the doors to be shut and not opened until the Sabbath was over. I stationed some of my own men at the gates so that no load could be brought in on the Sabbath day . . . Then I commanded the Levites to purify themselves and go and guard the gates in order to keep the Sabbath day holy.
>
> Remember me for this also, my God, and show mercy to me according to your great love.
>
> **Nehemiah 13:19, 22**

Some of the people in Judah had been bringing in loads of grain and other goods on the Sabbath day, a day on which Israelites were commanded by God not to work. Maybe people other than the

Israelites were driving the carts, but it was the Israelites who ended up unloading the grain. They may have known they were breaking the Sabbath, but could have easily thought, *We have no choice. The grain is here and has to be unloaded or it will be wasted.* They couldn't resist the temptation to work with the grain on the day it arrived.

So what did Nehemiah do? He planned in advance to keep the Sabbath by locking the doors so the grain couldn't be brought in. Don't miss the lessons here for rededication: we must plan in advance to *keep out of our lives the things that are hurting us.*

If you're struggling with alcohol addiction, you plan in advance to not go to a bar—even if it's just to hang out with your friends. If you're asking God to help you stay pure and not have sex before marriage, you don't pray for purity together in the backseat of your car. No, you plan in advance to not be in the car because you recognize what can easily happen in that situation.

Where in your life do you need to plan in advance so you don't put yourself in situations where you trip into the same sins again and again? How do you need to order the doors shut and then post guards over those areas of your life?

Fill Your Life with God's Purposes

The fourth step in rededication is to fill your life with God's purposes. As important as the first three steps in this process are, they will mean nothing unless you also take the fourth step. It's never enough to try to just keep out what's wrong; you must at the same time be filling your life with *doing what is right.* Nehemiah 13:30 reads, "So I purified the priests and the Levites of everything foreign, and assigned them duties, each to his own task." They needed to quit doing what was eroding their purpose by getting back to doing their God-given tasks.

The importance of this truth is captured in that old phrase, "Idle hands are the devil's playground." If we have spaces that are left empty in our lives, they tend to get filled with the wrong things. The greatest example of this in the Bible may well be King David. When all the kings were out to war, when he was supposed to be battling for his country, he decided to stay back in the city of Jerusalem—and when he was walking around on his palace roof, he saw Bathsheba and fell into sin (2 Samuel 11).

You don't flee temptation by sitting idly and waiting until it goes away. It's not going to go away. You run from temptation by running toward doing what's right. Second Timothy 2:22 reads, "Flee the evil desires of youth and pursue righteousness, faith, love and peace, along with those who call on the Lord out of a pure heart." You run away from what's wrong; you run toward what's right; and you run with those who also are pursuing purity.

Dedication is worth nothing as a feeling or a noble thought; it only shows its worth as a decision. Many people misunderstand what it is we are deciding. We are not deciding to "do good things" or to "be a good person." That's a self-defeating decision.

When we try to do good on our own power, we tend to either internally fight doing what's right and constantly fall for temptation, or feel we're doing a great job at doing what's right and fall into pride. It's the classic "sinner or Pharisee" dilemma—either way we've lost connection to the power God wants to give us. The secret is to stop trying to be dedicated and to instead trust God and let our dedication flow from that trust.

As we approach the end of our look at how to put it together again when it's all fallen apart, let's go back to the church in Marysville. It was one of the great privileges of my life to lead the people in that building project. Truth is, they often led me. There were more than a few times that I looked at the relatively small number of people in the church and felt I was leading them into a project we wouldn't be able to finish.

In those moments, they reminded me that I had been teaching them about faith and that they believed God could do great things. There's nothing quite so humbling as having your own sermons preached back at you! Because of their faith and sacrifice, after meeting for a few years in a community college, this small church bought five acres of land by a freeway and built a building so they could continue to serve the community.

Several months after we'd been in that new building, a pastor from our area—someone I'd never met—dropped by the church. He told me that the land we had built on had at one time been property his congregation had looked at purchasing. In fact, years before, he and his entire leadership team and come and knelt to pray on that then bare land.

They had dedicated the land to God's use and prayed specifically that God would allow a church to be built on that land. "The only problem," he told me, smiling, "is that we didn't pray that *our* church would be built on this land!" He went on to say that our building after the flood had become a great source of faith for his church, as they saw their prayers being answered in ways they had not expected.

That church stands on that property today as one testimony among millions to God's faithful work of rebuilding. His faithfulness never fails. His endurance never ends. As he completes his work of rebuilding a church, a business, a relationship, or a purpose in your life, you can continue to rely on his loving promise: "The God of heaven will give us success. We his servants will start rebuilding" (Nehemiah 2:20).

DEDICATE IT TO GOD:
My First Steps

Dedicate yourself to these seven principles for putting it together again by praying these commitments out loud:

1. I will find the strength to start.
2. I will take the first step.
3. I will appreciate others.
4. I will expect and reject opposition.
5. I will build on my successes.
6. I will celebrate to sustain my joy.
7. I will dedicate it to God.

Father, thank you that you will never give up on me when things fall apart. You're a God who shows up. Whether it seems like I have everything together or like everything is falling apart, you are there to strengthen me and show me the way. Instead of looking at my circumstances, I choose to look at you. God of heaven, I ask you to give success so that as your servant I will start rebuilding and stay rebuilding. I pray this in Jesus' name. Amen.

ACKNOWLEDGMENTS

I am grateful to the team at Zondervan, including John Sloan, Dirk Buursma, and Stan Gundry, for their faithful encouragement over the years.

I am grateful for the faith of God's people at Feather River Baptist Church, who were willing to encourage the faith of a still young pastor as we rebuilt together.

I am grateful as well for the courageous love of the followers of Jesus at Saddleback Church, who have shown me hundreds upon hundreds of examples of what it means to allow God to put something back together again.

Finally, grateful thanks to my wife, Chaundel, who strengthened me as we lived these truths and encouraged me in writing them out.

FIND THE STRENGTH TO START

CATCHING UP/LOOKING AHEAD

1. If you're meeting for the first time as a group, go around the room and share your name, where you were born, and something about your life.
2. What picture comes to your mind when you hear the word *rebuild*?

KEY VERSE

The God of heaven will give us success. We his servants will start rebuilding.

Nehemiah 2:20

VIDEO TEACHING

There is a different ten-minute video teaching with Tom for each week of this study. Watch this week's teaching together now at YouTube.com/TomHolladay.

DISCOVERY QUESTIONS

Remember, it's not vital to get to every question every week. The goal is to find just one question that prompts some good discussion and encouragement.

1. What is it that you would like to put together again?
2. How do you find yourself reacting to your problems right now—with faith, doubt, fear, anxiety, hope, or some other response?
3. Is there a place in your life where you are currently mourning a loss?
4. How has prayer helped you see an opportunity for faith? What do you do when you don't feel full of faith as you pray?

LIVING ON PURPOSE

God's five purposes for each of us are evangelism, discipleship, fellow-ship, ministry, and worship. In this section, we'll look at how we can take practical steps to fulfill one of those purposes based on the truths we've looked at in this study.

WORSHIP

Plan to do a one-day fast in the week ahead or to have a more extended time in prayer if you're not able to fast. Start by focusing on who God is and then open your heart to what he wants to impress on you about who you are.

A tip on this one: If all you're hearing are negatives about you, listen more closely. God is love, and he has words of encouragement as well as correction for his children.

PRAYING TOGETHER

Ask for God's strength and blessing in those "this is what I want to put together again" areas that each group member shared.

TAKE THE FIRST STEP

CATCHING UP/LOOKING AHEAD

1. Talk about what you experienced in your fasting or prayer times during this last week.
2. When you think about how a baby takes his or her first steps, what does it say to you about first steps in our lives as adults?

KEY VERSE

The king said to me, "What is it you want?"

Then I prayed to the God of heaven, and I answered the king, "If it pleases the king and if your servant has found favor in his sight, let him send me to the city in Judah where my ancestors are buried so that I can rebuild it."

Nehemiah 2:4–5

VIDEO TEACHING

You can watch a ten-minute video teaching with Tom on this week's truths at YouTube.com/TomHolladay.

DISCOVERY QUESTIONS

1. Is there some point where you already have taken—or still need to take—a stand for what God wants to rebuild?
2. What can you do to prepare for what you're dreaming God will do?
3. How have you seen God work to calm your fears as you've faced a risk of faith?
4. Is it easy or difficult for you to ask for help?

LIVING ON PURPOSE

God's five purposes for each of us are evangelism, discipleship, fellowship, ministry, and worship. In this section, we'll look at how we can take practical steps to fulfill one of those purposes based on the truths we've looked at in this study.

FELLOWSHIP

Who can stand with you as you rebuild? Who do you need to ask for help?

Start with this group and ask them to specifically pray for you. To see how God works during these seven weeks of meeting, start a group prayer request sheet.

PRAYING TOGETHER

Pray for the requests you shared a moment ago, as well as for other needs your group members might have.

APPRECIATE OTHERS

CATCHING UP/LOOKING AHEAD

1. Did you see any answers to prayer this last week?
2. Who is one of the most thankful people you know?

KEY VERSE

> How we thank God for you! Because of you we have great joy as we enter God's presence.
>
> **1 Thessalonians 3:9 NLT**

VIDEO TEACHING

You can watch a ten-minute video teaching with Tom on this week's truths at YouTube.com/TomHolladay.

DISCOVERY QUESTIONS

1. What person are you thankful for?
2. How have others' expressions of appreciation to you made an impact on your life?
3. What do you think would help you be more appreciative and get better at expressing appreciation to others?
4. What did this chapter say to you about how you express appreciation to God?

LIVING ON PURPOSE

God's five purposes for each of us are evangelism, discipleship, fellowship, ministry, and worship. In this section, we'll look at how we can take practical steps to fulfill one of those purposes based on the truths we've looked at in this study.

MINISTRY

Write a note of thanks and encouragement to someone each day this week.

PRAYING TOGETHER

Pray prayers of thanksgiving to God together as you end your group discussion.

EXPECT AND REJECT OPPOSITION

CATCHING UP/LOOKING AHEAD

1. Talk about your experiences of writing a thank-you note to someone each day (or even one day) this last week.
2. When you face opposition, is your first reaction to want to engage or to want to escape?

KEY VERSE

Therefore, put on every piece of God's armor so you will be able to resist the enemy in the time of evil. Then after the battle you will still be standing firm.

Ephesians 6:13 NLT

VIDEO TEACHING

You can watch a ten-minute video teaching with Tom on this week's truths at YouTube.com/TomHolladay.

DISCOVERY QUESTIONS

1. What helps you redirect your thoughts in the face of negative talk or gossip?
2. Is there a new strategy you need to consider in order to reposition your forces as you face some kind of attack on your faith, family, or business?
3. Is there an area of discouragement you're facing where the group could pray for you?
4. When you face distraction, what helps you regain your focus?

LIVING ON PURPOSE

God's five purposes for each of us are evangelism, discipleship, fellowship, ministry, and worship. In this section, we'll look at how we can take practical steps to fulfill one of those purposes based on the truths we've looked at in this study.

DISCIPLESHIP

Scripture memory has proven to be one of the keys to victory in the lives of many believers. Memorize the key verse for this week, or one of these verses that address the four strategies for winning the battle.

When you are ridiculed

Therefore, there is now no condemnation for those who are in Christ Jesus.

Romans 8:1

When you are attacked

We are hard pressed on every side, but not crushed; perplexed, but not in despair; persecuted, but not abandoned; struck down, but not destroyed.

2 Corinthians 4:8–9

When you are discouraged

Humble yourselves, therefore, under God's mighty hand, that he may lift you up in due time. Cast all your anxiety on him because he cares for you.

1 Peter 5:6–7

When you are distracted

I press on toward the goal to win the prize for which God has called me heavenward in Christ Jesus.

Philippians 3:14

PRAYING TOGETHER

Share and pray for one another's needs as you close your group meeting.

BUILD ON YOUR SUCCESSES

CATCHING UP/LOOKING AHEAD

1. Ask if anyone had a victory in the face of the opposition we inevitably face as we put things together again.
2. What God-given successes are you most grateful for?

KEY VERSE

So the wall was completed on the twenty-fifth of Elul, in fifty-two days.

When all our enemies heard about this, all the surrounding nations were afraid and lost their self-confidence, because they realized that this work had been done with the help of our God.

Nehemiah 6:15–16

VIDEO TEACHING

You can watch a ten-minute video teaching with Tom on this week's truths at YouTube.com/TomHolladay.

DISCOVERY QUESTIONS

1. As you read this chapter, did something come to mind that you could do to secure the investment you've put into rebuilding?
2. Who are the people in your support network?
3. Is there something you need to let go of in order to do all that God is asking you to do?
4. What hopes do you have for God to bless others through what he has rebuilt in your life?

LIVING ON PURPOSE

God's five purposes for each of us are evangelism, discipleship, fellowship, ministry, and worship. In this section, we'll look at how we can take practical steps to fulfill one of those purposes based on the truths we've looked at in this study.

MINISTRY

Our greatest ministry to others often comes out of our greatest struggles. Look for specific ways to encourage someone this week with the story of how God was with you as you sought to rebuild.

PRAYING TOGETHER

Take a moment to pray for one another's needs.

CELEBRATE TO SUSTAIN YOUR JOY

CATCHING UP/LOOKING AHEAD

1. Did you have the opportunity to encourage someone this week? Did God give you some ideas for a ministry to others that can grow out of what he is restoring in your life?
2. Would you rather celebrate quietly or celebrate loudly?

KEY VERSE

"The joy of the LORD is your strength."

Nehemiah 8:10

VIDEO TEACHING

You can watch a ten-minute video teaching with Tom on this week's truths at YouTube.com/TomHolladay.

DISCOVERY QUESTIONS

1. Is there someone you need to put things right with so you can deepen your celebration in worship?
2. Describe a time when the truth of God's Word shone out to you as you worshiped with others.
3. How have you found celebration in feasting, in sharing with others, or in stillness?
4. How do you relate to the following sentences from this chapter?

"You find yourself grinding away at spiritual habits, trying to become more powerful, when the real intent is that you become more joyful. Feeling powerful is not your strength; the joy of the Lord is your strength."

LIVING ON PURPOSE

God's five purposes for each of us are evangelism, discipleship, fellowship, ministry, and worship. In this section, we'll look at how we can take practical steps to fulfill one of those purposes based on the truths we've looked at in this study.

EVANGELISM

A burst of joy often comes when we share with someone else the good news of what God is doing in our lives. Go around the group and have each person share the name of someone they're praying for to begin a relationship with Christ.

In the week ahead, pray for these people whose names have been shared—that they will come to faith in the Lord Jesus.

PRAYING TOGETHER

Pray for this group of people you just mentioned and for one another's needs.

Talk about whether there is another book you'd like to read together and discuss after you finish this study next week.

DEDICATE IT TO GOD

CATCHING UP/LOOKING AHEAD

What has been most meaningful to you in what we have studied together during these seven weeks?

KEY VERSE

> Therefore, I urge you, brothers and sisters, in view of God's mercy, to offer your bodies as a living sacrifice, holy and pleasing to God—this is your true and proper worship.
>
> **Romans 12:1**

VIDEO TEACHING

You can watch a ten-minute video teaching with Tom on this week's truths at YouTube.com/TomHolladay.

DISCOVERY QUESTIONS

1. Are there ways you've discovered that help thankful joy take the lead in your life?
2. How have you seen purity expressed in what you pursue?
3. How have you personally experienced the truth that the greatest joy in life comes not from what you get but from what you give?
4. What are some specific places you'd like the group to pray for as you seek to keep your dedication refreshed?

LIVING ON PURPOSE

God's five purposes for each of us are evangelism, discipleship, fellowship, ministry, and worship. In this section, we'll look at how we can take practical steps to fulfill one of those purposes based on the truths we've looked at in this study.

WORSHIP

Spend some time this next week reviewing and thanking God for the truths that grow out of the book of Nehemiah. Dedicate yourself to living these truths through the power that God gives in Christ.

PRAYING TOGETHER

Pray for one another's needs.

As you finish this study, talk about whether there is another book you'd like to read together and discuss as a group.

The Relationship Principles of Jesus

Tom Holladay, teaching pastor, Saddleback Church

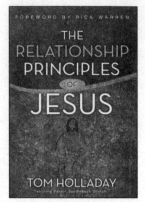

What would you give to radically improve, even transform, what matters most in your relationships?

How about forty days of your time?

In forty days, bring new depth and health to your marriage, your family, and your friendships. Six weeks to explore and implement six foundational principles that Jesus taught and lived. You'll be equipped with insights and a practical path for fulfilling God's intention for all your relationships—even the difficult ones.

Shaped after Rick Warren's monumental bestseller, *The Purpose Driven® Life*, this book invites you to learn from the Master of relationships. *The Relationship Principles of Jesus* will profoundly shape how you view relationships.